# EARLY ENGLISH READING THEORY

STUDIES IN RHETORIC/COMMUNICATION
Carroll C. Arnold, *Series Editor*

Richard B. Gregg
*Symbolic Inducement and Knowing:*
*A Study in the Foundations of Rhetoric*

Richard A. Cherwitz and James W. Hikins
*Communication and Knowledge:*
*An Investigation in Rhetorical Epistemology*

Herbert W. Simons and Aram A. Aghazarian, Editors
*Form, Genre, and the Study of Political Discourse*

Walter R. Fisher
*Human Communication as Narration:*
*Toward a Philosophy of Reason, Value, and Action*

David Payne
*Coping with Failure:*
*The Therapeutic Uses of Rhetoric*

# Early English Reading Theory:

## ORIGINS OF CURRENT DEBATES

by David Bartine

*University of South Carolina Press*

For Jane, Jennifer, Alexis, Julia,
for V and K Edwards,
and in memory of Don Geiger

Copyright © University of South Carolina 1989

Published in Columbia, South Carolina, by the
University of South Carolina Press

Manufactured in the United States of America


First Edition

Library of Congress Cataloging-in-Publication Data

Bartine, David E.
  Early English reading theory : origins of current debates / by
David Bartine.—1st ed.
    p.    cm.—(Studies in rhetoric/communication)
  Bibliography: p.
  Includes index.
  ISBN 0-87249-592-2
  1. Reading—Philosophy—History.   2. Reading, Psychology of—
History.   3. Reading comprehension—Philosophy—History.
I. Title.   II. Series.
LB1050.2.B37   1989
428.4′01—dc19                                                    88-20910
                                                                      CIP

# CONTENTS

# EDITOR'S FOREWORD

Behind the query, "Why can't Johnny read?" lies a more basic question: What *is* it to "read" English? In *English Reading Theory*, David Bartine isolates fundamental master questions that a useful theory of reading must articulate and answer. He also fills a void in historical accounts of Anglo-American rhetorical studies. Most students of literature and rhetoric are unaware that thoughtful theorists and pedagogues struggled two centuries ago to construct a theory of what it is to read a text written in English. Professor Bartine rescues these thinkers from obscurity and reports the variety of ways in which they tried to solve the still-pressing problem of how to render literate a populace confronted with widely disseminated popular, literary, and scientific writing. He shows that their trials and errors contain lessons for moderns who still struggle with the same problem.

Bartine's history shows the importance of blending sophisticated theory of rhetoric with sophisticated theory of grammar in constructing a conception of how Jenny or Johnny might read effectively. Bartine's study also demonstrates why to ask what it is to read is to ask questions about the literary, rhetorical, grammatical, and even "oratorical" activities of those who use the English language. The study illustrates, too, the importance of deciding precisely how, if at all, written and spoken forms of a language resemble and differ from one another.

Bartine makes a strong argument, based on his historical research, that pragmatic principles yield richer and more profitable understandings of written or oral communication than do aesthetic principles. In response to the familiar dichotomies of style versus content and form versus substance, Bartine argues specifically that in a theory of how communication is best assimilated, "style" needs to be conceived as authorial *strategy* devised to communicate ideas and emotions to situated

vi

audiences. This position is consonant with the work of modern rhetorical theorists such as Richard M. Weaver, Kenneth Burke, and Chaim Perelman, who have contended, in Burke's language, that symbolic communications are "answers to questions posed by the situation in which they arose." They are "*strategic* answers, *stylized* answers," and they must be read and heard as such if they are to be understood fully.

Carroll C. Arnold
Editor, *Rhetoric/Communication*
*University of South Carolina Press*

# PREFACE

The main purpose of this book is to tell the story of the evolution of eighteenth- and early nineteenth-century British reading theory and pedagogy. The pertinence of the study lies in the fact that during the latter half of the twentieth century, speculation about reading has, without benefit of sufficient hindsight, returned to many issues that were explored two centuries earlier.

We have heard for several years that there is a reading crisis in American education, and we have also heard a variety of proposals for reform, including the ever-present slogan "Back to basics!" We have also heard for several years debates about the activity of reading and its "objects," and we have seen proposals that have challenged us to rethink all of our assumptions about the "basics" to which reading should return.

Debates about the current quality of reading are no longer confined to academic publications. In a recent *Washington Post* article, Charles Griswold, Jr., summarized a few of the issues in what he called a debate "of historic proportions." Griswold recognized that once we ask the "seemingly innocuous question: 'What does it mean to read?' " we have started down the path toward a thicket of questions about "meaning" and about what he refers to as some of "the most basic philosophical issues."

The current debates are of historic proportions not only because they have serious consequences for the future, but also because they have a history. That history has gone largely unrecognized, yet it can be instructive to participants in modern versions of the debate. The eighteenth- and early nineteenth-century English phase of that history is the primary concern of this book.

# ACKNOWLEDGMENTS

An early form of my discussion of Smart appeared in my article " 'Key-Word' Theories of Reading: From Elocution to Interpretation," in *Performance of Literature,* edited by David W. Thompson (New York: University Press of America, 1983).

I have had the generous support of many people in the preparation of this study. Professor Robert W. Rogers aided me early in the project and provided a most helpful critique of the final version. Professors Michael Conlon, Albert Tricomi, Thomas Conley, and Alvin Vos have labored with me through versions of the manuscript. I am grateful to all for their invaluable advice. To these colleagues and others, including Richard McLain, I express my appreciation.

I also want to thank Carol Fischler, Chris Storrs, Peg Petcovsky, Barbara Walling, Sylvia White, and Lisa Fegley-Schmidt, who introduced me to, and guided me through, the magical world of word processing.

The aid of Carroll Arnold was vital in transforming this project from manuscript to book. Those who have worked with him know his wisdom, his wit, and his remarkable ability to lead a writer to see what must be seen. I am indebted to him for his contributions and guidance.

D. B.

# EARLY ENGLISH READING THEORY

# INTRODUCTION

The recent surge of interest in reading theory is shared by students having a wide range of academic backgrounds. Rhetoric, literary criticism, interpretation, linguistics, education, and psychology are among the disciplines animating current, and often controversial, explorations of reading. Interdisciplinary study of the subject has raised a variety of issues about which there has been considerable disagreement. All theorists and critics, however, seem to share hostility toward any view of reading "whose preconceptions about how to read, and what to read for, are so fundamental that they remain unvoiced and unthought, and thus appear 'natural', 'intuitive', free of theory."[1]

Among basic issues in reading theory are problems about text, authorial intention, meaning, and figuration. The identification of these problems has involved examining and re-examining assumptions about texts, meaning, and the reader's role in the act of reading. The conception of a reader as a passive receiver has unquestionably been put to rest. The questions that remain in doubt, and that drive current debates about reading theory, are those about the acts a reader performs—how gaps are filled in, how meanings are completed, and how meanings are created by readers.

An unfortunate concomitant of the recent interest in theories of reading has been a notion that little sophisticated thought was given to the study of reading prior to the second half of the twentieth century. However, the corpus of early and often sophisticated work on reading and pedagogy for readers plainly shows that between 1710 and 1840 theorists examined and debated numerous fundamental issues that continue to attract study and attention. A broader understanding of the history of these inquiries into the nature of readers and reading can yield profitable guidelines for present-day theorizing and pedagogy.

1

Three major considerations justify an intensive examination of theory of reading as it emerged in the eighteenth and early nineteenth centuries. First, in that period as now, the interest in reading was highly interdisciplinary. Contributors to theory building then, as now, were deeply concerned with rhetoric, literary criticism, linguistics, psychology, and pedagogy. Then, as now, there was debate concerning the relative usefulness of aesthetic and pragmatic analyses of texts and of reading as process; a "unit of meaning" in ongoing discourse was variously defined; and theorists struggled with the relations of thought to language and of spoken language to written language.

Second, these early scholars were pioneers who came afresh to the problems of how to read and how to teach people to read, bringing with them fewer preconceptions than moderns have about what it is to read. By and large they were educators who were seeking to understand in a sophisticated and teachable way what they, their peers, and their students accomplished through communication and identification with authors. These writers asked, for the first time, how reading the English language was carried on and how it could be carried on better. They addressed these questions with few well-established precedents and few predisposing theoretical constructs. We therefore have the opportunity to see how these theorists and pedagogues picked up, and often from necessity discarded, conceptions borrowed from the intellectual milieu in which they lived. Through the century-and-a-quarter in which theory of reading English was a subject of intellectual ferment, a number of explanations of reading that are still current were tried and their values and limitations discovered.

A third reason for this inquiry is to revise historical records by calling attention to the work of some writers whose work deserves far greater attention than it has received. Hans Aarsleff, Stephen Land, and Murray Cohen have retrieved from obscurity some significant eighteenth-century language studies that were previously overlooked or misconstrued because they did not fit tidily within the confines of twentieth-century histories of linguistics.[2] In a comparable way, we should reexamine a number of eighteenth-century works on reading that have remained obscure in part because their authors' diverse interests have made it difficult to place them squarely in the lineage of any particular academic discipline.

Precisely what is meant by the term "to read" is not now, and was not in the eighteenth century, self-evident. One modern dictionary definition of "to read" runs: "to peruse and apprehend the meaning of (something written, printed, etc.): *to read a book.*" This primitive definition identifies two major subjects of concern to any student of reading: the act of perusal and the act of understanding. The second of these acts was vigorously discussed by eighteenth- and early nineteenth-century writers, as it is by their counterparts today. Then, as now, the question, What is it to understand something written? immediately gave rise to the still more perplexing question, What is "meaning" and where is it found?

Another modern dictionary definition of the verb points up a problem that created special difficulties for eighteenth-century scholars. This definition characterizes "to read" as "to utter aloud or render in speech (something written or printed, etc.): *reading a story to children.*" This interpretation of "reading" has been troublesome in the evaluation of the eighteenth-century writers on reading, some of whom were and have been considered almost exclusively as teachers of oral reading. These writers have been viewed by modern scholars as constituting the "elocutionary movement" within the history of rhetoric, a movement often treated as being solely devoted to the rhetorical canon of delivery. Such an interpretation of the elocutionists' work led one major historian of rhetoric, Wilbur Samuel Howell, to the enigmatic conclusion that the elocutionists "endorsed a futureless idea that was destined against logic and common sense to have a two-hundred-year future in England and America."[3] I do not propose to discuss this statement, but I do propose to show that some elocutionists had considerable influence in the evolution of a coherent theory of reading, taken as perusal and understanding, as well as utterance. Accordingly, some writers on reading who traditionally have been grouped under the label "elocutionists" receive a more sympathetic hearing here than has been given them by Howell and some other historians of rhetoric. Further, it is a hearing largely distinct from that given them by writers on the history of oral interpretation.

In fact, it is precisely the relationship of perusal and comprehension on the one hand to the act of utterance on the other that comes under close scrutiny in the work of several eighteenth-century writers on reading. Granted, this relationship was more intensely considered in the eighteenth century than it has been in our own time, but contemporary students of reading can profit by reviewing the issues their predecessors raised about this question. It is still not definitively settled whether written English is one language and spoken English a different language, or whether both are forms of the same language.

A further justification for examining eighteenth- and early nineteenth-century deliberations on the nature of reading is suggested by the observations of George A. Miller, a modern scientific student of communication and information theory. Says Miller, "The study of reading comprehension is more than a study of how a reader extracts information by decoding, parsing, and interpreting a text." Miller believes that reading for comprehension is a form of "problem solving" in which readers "relate the textual concept they are synthesizing to their general store of knowledge and belief."[4] His observations draw attention to problems in theory of reading that early writers addressed directly and that contemporary theorists must also cope with: What kinds of knowledge and belief does or should a reader bring to a given work or to texts in general? Is all reading "problem solving" in Miller's sense, or are there different kinds of reading? Such questions concern the options and responsibilities of readers, and they confront one directly with fundamental questions about the status of texts, their forms of control or lack of control over readers' perceptions and interpretations, and the degree of liberty "permitted" to readers as interpreters. All of these issues arose in eighteenth- and early nineteenth-century writers' discussions of reading. Some of these writers ultimately concluded that both principles of syntax and principles of rhetorical structure had to be incorporated in a coherent, pragmatic theory of reading. But whether and how comprehension relates to the evaluation and appreciation of texts was not settled for theory of reading by the mid-nineteenth century, nor is it settled today. The past can show us some of the reasons for this continuing difficulty.

In recent years an important controversy in studies of literary criticism has concerned the separability or inseparability of interpretation and criticism. For example, E. D. Hirsch, Jr., helped set the stage for dramatic exchanges when he undertook the overthrow of "the idea that interpretation is criticism and vice versa." Hirsch took this position:

> Understanding (and therefore interpretation, in the strict sense of the word) is both logically and psychologically prior to what is generally called criticism. It is true that this distinction between understanding and evaluation cannot always show itself in the finished work of criticism—nor, perhaps, should it—but a general grasp and acceptance of the distinction might help correct some of the most serious faults of current criticism (its subjectivism and relativism) and might even make it plausible to think of literary study as a corporate enterprise and a progressive discipline.[5]

Eighteenth-century students of reading focused directly on whether the activity of critical reading should be construed as a discipline in its own right and with its own principles—a discipline strictly separable from reading for comprehension. Jane Tompkins is one commentator who has noted two disparate views of literature that contributed to an eighteenth-century debate about critical reading. On the one hand there were writers who construed the work of art "as an event in the social world with social consequences for author and audience." On the other there were those for whom critical reading was viewed as a "science" whose object was "literary experience . . . seen as occupying a realm of its own, one whose frame of reference, in R. S. Crane's phrase, is 'not the republic, but the republic of letters.' "[6] Reviewing the arguments among early scholars who held these different commitments, twentieth-century scholars who either support or dispute Hirsch's position will, at the very least, recognize their allies and foes in this conceptual heritage.

The eighteenth-century debates about basic reading and critical reading also show how commitment to one or another of these kinds of reading implies unique features for pedagogy—assumptions about the levels of reading ability a populace can be expected to reach and about what needs to be taught if readers are to be brought to one or another level of competency in reading. Understanding how pioneers in theory of reading coped with these issues is certainly relevant in an age in which "Why Johnny Can't Read" is a slogan and "critical thinking" an instance of academic jargon.

Eighteenth- and early nineteenth-century thinking about reading was, as I have said, strikingly interdisciplinary. Moreover, several of these early writers were searching their way toward a systematic discipline. Hans Aarsleff, Stephen Land, Murray Cohen, and Stephen Toulmin in his *Human Understanding* have called attention to the dangers of allowing one's judgment of past intellectual activity to be colored by the operating principles of a particular discipline as those principles are understood in present-day intellectual life.[7] Toulmin in particular has suggested that the most comprehensive and reliable approach to interdisciplinary activity is to focus on the questions that are shared in the intellectual activities one explores.

Toulmin's approach, which I follow, is particularly applicable to the inquiry I am undertaking. Insofar as theory of reading is concerned, the period from 1710 to 1840 was an era of searching for answers to basic questions about fairly commonplace, communicative activity. The searchers, with their varied intellectual orientations, nimbly worked through a number of divergent, sometimes contradictory assumptions and postulates about reading. In the process they carried out an ongoing dialogue and debate concerning the issues and problems that they jointly recognized as needing solutions.

The broad pattern of that dialogue was one in which the thinkers began with fixed and sometimes contrary views of language as a phenomenon, of the relations between oral and silent reading, and of the nature of "units" of communicative thought and meaning. By the end of the period, the most original and vigorous thinkers had arrived at the outline and some of the details of a coherent, though not entirely comprehensive, theory of reading written discourses. The dominant theory had moved from the exploration of reading words through the examination of reading sentences to the study of reading discourses as wholes. These thinkers had not, by 1840, achieved what Toulmin calls a "compact discipline": "a rational enterprise whose conceptual repertory is exposed at every stage to critical reappraisal and modification in the light of clearly recognized and agreed collective ideals." However, they showed a strong impulse toward constructing a discipline of reading, that is, drawing principles, concepts, and procedures out of a variety of existing intellectual enterprises and organizing them into a discipline of reading. The record shows, at a good many moments during this period, that while these writers agreed not necessarily on answers, they did agree on questions that needed to be asked and answered. Thus eighteenth- and early-nineteenth-century thought about reading constituted what Toulmin calls a "would-be discipline" in which there were signs of a "diffuse discipline."[8]

In the eighteenth century, as in our own time, a good deal of thinking about reading was motivated by the goal of making available to the public the principles of reading for comprehension and the principles of judgment about matters read. In other words, there was ambition to enable people to understand, enjoy, and evaluate what they read and to assist them in passing that understanding, enjoyment, and judgment on to others. In the first stage of the study of reading, textbooks on reading treated the subject as relatively unproblematic. Indeed, the first such textbook of the century was something of a footnote to what the author considered a more pressing task. Nonetheless, thinkers swiftly acknowledged that reading effectively was a complex matter. One of the special values of tracing the development of eighteenth-century thought about reading is that we can observe how thoughtful writers attempted to deal with problems successively revealed to them precisely because they were trying to build and refine theory and ground pedagogical practice upon it. The problems they unearthed were therefore of two types, pedagogical and theoretical.

Because the earliest writers on reading aimed at creating literate citizens, pedagogical problems often were faced before theoretical considerations came into focus. Several of the early works concentrated purely on making people competent readers. These works concerned themselves with specific techniques for instructing students in basic principles of comprehending and judging what was read. They raised questions about the sort of background instruction that could be assumed, the level at which instruction should begin, and how much students of reading should be exposed to reading theory.

Almost inevitably questions about pedagogy arose, and they were in turn virtually subsumed by questions about the theory of reading. It is scarcely an exaggeration to say that at the beginning of the eighteenth century no theory of reading existed. The theoretical questions that arose during the century were basic. First these thinkers asked, From which established intellectual enterprises should theorists and pedagogues borrow models and principles in developing reading as an independent study? The most prominent answers given to this question advised borrowing principles and methods of understanding and appreciating the written word from logic, rhetoric, grammar, and biblical interpretation. Suggestions that principles and methods be borrowed from these studies led naturally enough to discussions of how these established studies or subjects were to be construed. The question of how rhetoric was to be understood, and of what ought and ought not to be borrowed from it, had special prominence during much of this period. As will be made clear in the chapters to follow, the natures and functions of tropes and figures were prominently discussed topics.

As thinkers approached reading more theoretically, they also were forced to ask themselves, What are the principles of understanding and judgment? Are these principles so closely related that training in one process will instill the other? Or are understanding and judgment such different processes that each must be inculcated separately?

Partly because inherited rhetorical doctrines were closely associated with oral communication, and partly because reading aloud was considered by some the consummate achievement of an art of reading, another question arose: What relationships hold or do not hold between principles of intelligent and artistic oral reading and reading silently for comprehension and judgment? This inquiry led to heated debates about what spoken and written language can and cannot convey. It also promoted questions about the extent to which understanding and art in one form of reading translate into understanding and art in the other. Such issues were especially sensitive in the eighteenth century because oral reading in schools and homes was far more common than those activities are in the twentieth century, yet the issues discussed are still relevant to contemporary theories of language and communication.

One has only to contrast the modern views of Walter Ong and others with those of Hirsch and Jacques Derrida to see that closure concerning the importance of orality to literacy has still not been achieved. Ong holds the position that "written texts all have to be related somehow, directly or indirectly, to the world of sound, the natural habitat of language, to yield their meanings."[9] Against this view are lodged the contentions of such scholars as Hirsch and Derrida that the written form of language stands independent of the spoken form and has its own distinct systematicness.[10] A similar division of opinion was apparent among eighteenth-century writers on reading, and noting how that division first arose and what arguments were mustered for each view of language and meaning reminds us that these differences in points of view are not peculiar to our own times.

I said earlier that I follow Toulmin's lead in examining the interdisciplinary discussions of reading in the eighteenth and early nineteenth centuries. To do this requires consideration of how writers on reading dealt with a series of what I call "master questions," which any theory of reading must confront and which identify fundamental problems whose existence the early writers all acknowledged. Each of the early theorists answered these questions differently, much as modern theorists do; still all competent theory builders must consciously or unconsciously take positions on these questions. These master questions are questions about meaning, what it is, how it is conveyed, and what interactive roles writers and readers play. Furthermore, behind anyone's positions on such questions lurk identifiable epistemological assumptions. This early period began under the strong influence of John Locke's assumptions about signs and their meanings, but these assumptions underwent modifications when writers began to think intensely about "units of meaning" for readers.

A fuller understanding of early reading theory contributes to our understanding of the history of rhetoric in the eighteenth and early nineteenth centuries, for numerous eighteenth-century writers turned to rhetorical theory to borrow principles and tools for reading theory. Their interpretations of and borrowings from rhetorical doctrines largely had to do with figurative language and idiomatic usages that were treated as commonplaces of communication in English. Accounts of the history of rhetoric in the eighteenth century have suggested that figures and commonplaces were always viewed as "ornaments" of style. However, the record of rhetorical borrowings in eighteenth-century studies of reading shows that this interpretation of figuration was not universal. Builders of a theory of reading soon came to treat figures and commonplaces as strategic instrumentalities available to writers as commonly understood procedures by which to communicate pragmatically with readers.

The eighteenth-century shift from a focus on ornamentation to a focus on the pragmatics of conveying meaning through form has its contemporary counterpart, as Geoffrey Hartman indicates in *The Fate of Reading.* Hartman asks, "To what can we turn now to restore reading, or that conscious and scrupulous form of it we call literary criticism?" His answer is an echo, in modern terms, of answers given by some reading theorists of the late eighteenth and early nineteenth centuries:

> The advance that has occurred is mainly in the area of theory of convention, as it rules both reading and writing. The movement sparked by Jakobson, for example, though based on modern psychology and linguistics, can still be linked to the prescriptive criticism of the rhetorical schools from Antiquity on, which established a store of 'devices' to regulate the character, and assure the success, of the work of art. These rules or devices served to build a community of literate people, where all were potentially writers or orators. That this historical rhetoric has its productive as well as prescriptive side is clear when we think, for example, of Erasmus's *copia* method, or Lessing's *Essay on Fables,* with their literary formulae that could motivate new narratives as well as analyze existing ones. Those who are presently expanding and rationalizing the historical study of rhetoric in the hope of evolving a scientific 'grammar' on the level of poetics, are fulfilling, in my view, more of a communitarian than a scientific function: this grammar of forms, more systematic than Northrop Frye's, and as eminently teachable, should enable reading to gain back its anticipatory (but not necessarily prescriptive) vigor.[11]

Today those who explore the parameters of reading and the possibility of borrowing principles and tools from other disciplines, especially from rhetoric, should find it informative to observe their predecessors' borrowings, as well as the successes and shortcomings those borrowings had for theories of reading. As Hartman's statement indicates, the issue of where and what to borrow in building a theory of reading is by no means dormant.

NOTES TO INTRODUCTION

1. Robert Young, *Untying the Text* (London: Routledge and Kegan Paul, 1981), p. viii.

2. Hans Aarsleff, *The Study of Language in England, 1780–1860* (Princeton, N.J.: Princeton University Press, 1967), and *From Locke to Saussure: Essays on the Study of Language and Intellectual History* (Minneapolis: University of Minnesota Press, 1982). Stephen K. Land, *From Signs to Propositions* (Toronto: University of Toronto Press, 1971). Murray Cohen, *Sensible Words: Linguistic Practice in England, 1640–1785* (Baltimore, Md.: The Johns Hopkins University Press, 1974).

3. Wilbur Samuel Howell, *Eighteenth-Century British Logic and Rhetoric* (Princeton, N.J.: Princeton University Press, 1971), p. 146. For more sympathetic hearings of some of the same writers, see Wallace Bacon's "The Elocutionary Career of Thomas Sheridan, 1719–1788," *Speech Monographs* 31 (March 1964) 1–53, and T. O. Sloane's article on the history of rhetoric in the *Encyclopaedia Britannica, 1976.*

4. George A. Miller, "Images and Models, Similies and Metaphors," in *Metaphor and Thought,* ed. Andrew Ortony (Cambridge: Cambridge University Press, 1979), p. 209.

5. E. D. Hirsch, Jr., *Validity in Interpretation* (New Haven, Conn.: Yale University Press, 1967), p. 209.

6. Jane Tompkins, "The Reader in History," in *Reader Response Criticism,* ed. Jane Tompkins (Baltimore, Md.: The Johns Hopkins University Press, 1980), pp. 215–16.

7. Stephen Toulmin, *Human Understanding: The Collective Use and Evolution of Concepts* (Princeton, N.J.: Princeton University Press, 1972).

8. Toulmin, *Human Understanding,* pp. 378ff.

9. Walter J. Ong, *Orality and Literacy* (London: Methuen, 1982), p. 8.

10. E. D. Hirsch, Jr., *The Philosophy of Composition* (Chicago: University of Chicago Press, 1977), pp. 34ff.

11. Geoffrey H. Hartman, *The Fate of Reading* (Chicago: University of Chicago Press, 1975), p. 273.

# THE SHAPING OF
# EIGHTEENTH-CENTURY
# READING THEORY

This chapter characterizes some of the major forces that shaped eighteenth- and early nineteenth-century theory and pedagogy and introduces the issues with which eighteenth-century writers on reading had to contend, by exploring the historical context out of which these issues arose. First I treat some of the pressing social circumstances that generated a perceived need for the would-be discipline of reading. Then I examine some of the intellectual forces that affected the would-be discipline, noticing eighteenth-century reactions and contributions to the long-standing debates between the "ancients" and the "moderns." Examining these disputes as they were carried out in intellectual enterprises such as rhetoric, grammar, and biblical interpretation requires close scrutiny of the series of master questions I outlined in the introduction, especially the question, To which established intellectual enterprises should one turn to borrow principles for an independent study of reading?

## A PUBLIC FOR READING: THE NEED FOR
## BASIC INSTRUCTION

By the end of the seventeenth century, mounting supplies of reading material in English had created an extensive public demand for instruction in reading. Among the events generating this unprecedented abundance of reading material was the lapsing of the Printing Act in 1694 and the ensuing development of the provincial press. As W. H. G. Armytage observes, "in Norwich (1701), Bristol (1702), Exeter (1703), Shrewsbury (1704), Liverpool, Newcastle, Nottingham and Stamford (all in

1710) newspapers began to appear. There were 24 by 1723 and 130 by 1760."[1]

Ironically, this plenitude of reading matter was met by a pronounced shortage of readers. Several forces contributed to this shortage. Among them was a school "system" that, having increasingly recognized the value of the vernacular, had yet to find the means to train the general public in the fundamentals of reading and writing English. While the presence of new literary journals and a daily press no longer confined to London promised a spread of knowledge to the public at large, expansion of education in the second half of the seventeenth century from "endowed grammar school" to "endowed English school" still failed to provide most people with a rudimentary education.[2]

In an attempt to redress the readership problem, educators in late seventeenth-century England initiated a vigorous effort to extend the rudiments of education to those who did not have access to the limited number of grammar and English schools. Much of their effort has been described by historians as the "charity school movement," which contributed to the development of thousands of schools throughout Great Britain in the eighteenth century. The approach to reading offered in the "literary curriculum" of charity schools was characterized by M. G. Jones in the following manner:

> Reading lessons began with the letters of the alphabet, and went on, by the alphabetic-spelling method, to "the true spelling of words and the use of stops." The reading-book for these infant scholars, whose ages ranged upward of six years, was the Anglican catechism. . . . From the catechism the children were transferred to the Book of Common Prayer, in which they learnt to read the daily offices of the Liturgy, the Common Prayer for Morning and Evening, the Collects, and the Athanasian and Nicene Creeds. These were followed by Psalms of David in the Prayer Book version.[3]

Critics of charity school education objected to this method of instruction in reading. Jones summed up their complaints about the method of instruction when he noted that "correct pronunciation, rather than clear understanding," was the test of knowledge.[4] In 1792 Sarah Trimmer lodged a series of objections to charity school education, chief among which were the following:

> When the scholars leave school to go out into the world as servants or apprentices, a Bible, Common Prayer Book, and *Whole Duty of*

*Man* are given to them, and it is supposed, from the years they have been at school, that they must necessarily be furnished with a competent share of Christian knowledge to enable them to read with advantage and improvement as long as they live.[5]

Charity school instruction, with its flaws, characterized the education in reading possessed by a significant segment of the eighteenth-century British population. This prompted Isaac Watts and other writers to complain that people were rendered intent on the pronunciation of words but had little understanding of the material they "read." In the early part of the eighteenth century, these writers also lamented the narrow range of reading material offered to students. The charity school movement was, however, significant in another way in the evolution of reading as a subject of study. As many scholars have recognized, the system's use of religious reading material was a direct reflection of the Protestant Reformation's stress on individual familiarity with sacred texts, an emphasis that implied an allied notion that reading was "the birthright of all."[6] The massive charity school movement with its reading curriculum was a response to and a symbol of belief in reading as a divinely endorsed *right*.

Outside the charity school curriculum, training in reading English fared little better. The tradition of sending a child to "Petty School" for instruction in the rudiments of English before entering grammar school, where Latin was studied, was another way of training the public to read English. However, the weaknesses of Petty School education were manifest. In the mid-seventeenth century, Charles Hoole reported that "the want of good teachers of English in most places where grammar schools are erected causeth that many children are brought thither to learn the Latin tongue before they can read well."[7] This charge echoed through the eighteenth century. The paucity of trained elementary instructors was a situation that some of the later reading manuals were designed to correct.

Even in the forward-looking curricula of the few non-Anglican, "dissenting" academies that had been established by the late seventeenth century, attention to the study of English was slight. Daniel Defoe tempered with criticism his enthusiasm for the caliber of education offered at the dissenting academies of his time: "From our schools we have abundance of instances of men that come away masters of Science, critics in Greek and Hebrew, perfect in Languages and perfectly ignorant of their mother tongue."[8] Isaac Watts, and later Joseph Priestley, were prominent "dissenters" who worked to rectify the situation described by Defoe.

While Great Britain in the late seventeenth century had begun to expose a wider segment of its population to the rudiments of reading English, it had long been the case that relatively few of it citizens received instruction to prepare them to comprehend a variety of reading material. Some well-schooled private tutors and a few grammar school curricula did try to use exercises such as translation to encourage students to keep up their English as they studied other languages. Nonetheless, by the beginning of the eighteenth century several writers perceived that new theoretical as well as pedagogical inquiry was required to ameliorate the shortcomings of the prevailing modes of teaching students to read English.

## THE NEED FOR TRAINING IN CRITICAL READING

The wide availability of reading material and public interest in reading brought into focus another dimension of the need for theoretical and pedagogical investigation of reading. Some writers thought it was not sufficient to address the problems of basic comprehension. Several perceived a pressing need to create and offer instruction that would enable the public to read in a discriminating manner, to read critically, and to read according to the principles of "taste." John Dennis, Alexander Pope, and Charles Gildon shared a fear "that the rise of a reading public, uneducated, and avid for amusement, would destroy all the bases of taste."[9] Also, a desire for "polite learning" began to manifest itself among the general public. This desire was to contribute to the success of Defoe's *Review* and the enterprises of Joseph Addison and Richard Steele.

The wish to foster a critically astute reading public engendered one of the most intricate debates faced by eighteenth-century writers on reading. Some believed that principles of comprehension and of critical reading were inextricably linked. They argued that the principles needed to be tied together in a single discipline. Others thought there must be a strict separation of concern with principles of basic comprehension from concern with principles of critical reading. Here was a manifestation of one of the master questions: Are principles of understanding and principles of judgment so closely related that they must be entertained together, or are they so highly separable that they require distinct treatments? Differing responses to this question informed eighteenth- and nineteenth-century arguments over the status of literary criticism.

When we turn from social forces to consider the intellectual forces that affected the would-be discipline of reading, there comes into view the ancients-versus-moderns controversy, the battle of the books. The issue concerning the nature of principles of understanding and principles of judgment arose from intellectual changes that were taking place in the literary world. In *Concepts of Criticism* René Wellek notes that during the Renaissance, "grammarian, critic, philologist are almost interchangeable terms for the men engaged in the great enterprise of the revival of antiquity."[10] By the beginning of the eighteenth century, however, the harmony among the terms had been shattered, and the new dissonance was suggestive of one of the major struggles in the ancients-versus-moderns controversy. As Joseph M. Levine has asserted, "the very success of humanist grammarians and rhetoricians in recovering and elucidating the ancient authors" had, by the eighteenth century, resulted in an unexpected opposition in which the older "grammatical criticism," which had come to be known as "philology," found itself in the camp of the moderns, across the field of battle from the new "ancients," who were the defenders of eloquence and polite learning.[11] The fray was more than a mere struggle over the term "criticism." From the point of view of the new ancients and those committed to polite learning, criticism needed to be wrested away from philology, purified, and made to sustain the sense retrieved for it by John Dryden, who had returned to Aristotle to define criticism as " 'a standard of judging well.' "[12]

Within the ancients-versus-moderns battle were skirmishes over questions about what the ancients' new criticism, conceived as a standard of judging well, should discard and what it should keep from the moderns' philology. Was criticism to abandon everything associated with the methods of philology? Should it maintain some of the techniques associated with the older, once-venerated concept of grammatical criticism and reject modern philology's application of those techniques? Answers given to these and similar questions show some of the complexity of the ancients-versus-moderns battle in criticism. Moreover, these answers identify elements of struggles between classicism and romanticism.

The answers given by writers on reading to the question concerning principles of comprehension and principles of judgment ranged from harsh disavowals of philological inquiry to sophisticated warnings that the battle between the ancients and moderns may have dangerously simplified a complex set of considerations concerning the nature of reading. Some writers on reading saw the battle of the books as contributing to unfortunate educational fragmentation. They attempted to mend that fragmentation by returning to and reworking the classical models of rhetorical training. Several saw classical rhetorical training as a unified and adaptable kind of study in which understanding and judgment were companions in the stages through which a student passed on the way to eloquence. However, those who sought to reclaim the classical model disagreed about what blend of classical rhetoric's orality and literacy dimensions best suited the needs of a relatively young print culture.

Responding to the master question, To which established intellectual enterprises should one turn to borrow principles for an independent study of reading? writers wittingly and unwittingly took debatable stands about the place and functions of criticism. They could and did answer this master question by asserting that reading theory should borrow heavily from grammar, that reading theory should borrow heavily from one or another form of biblical criticism, that reading theory should borrow heavily from rhetoric, and that reading theory should borrow from some combination of principles drawn from all of these established disciplines. But any of these positions implied a theory of reading that was highly charged. Any theory of reading would be identified with one or another position in the battle of the ancients-versus-the moderns, given the intellectual climate of the eighteenth century. A theory of what it is to read had to evolve within a framework of controversy about the very nature of critical judgment.

Eighteenth- and early nineteenth-century writers on reading became involved in several controversies that were of long standing in the rhetorical and grammatical traditions. Two especially significant points of disagreement having to do with rhetoric concerned "method" and "style." A third controversy belonged largely to the grammatical tradition; it concerned the nature and locus of meaning.

## DISAGREEMENTS ABOUT METHOD: RHETORIC AND THE STUDY OF READING

Method, *dispositio,* or arrangement, the second of the five procedural "canons" of rhetoric, was traditionally treated as concerned with the proper and effective distribution of previously discovered material. One of the most controversial treatments of method prior to the eighteenth century was that associated with Ramism. Ramus's influential observations had drawn the attention but not the applause of Francis Bacon. In *The Advancement of Learning* Bacon identified "Elocution or tradition," or "Delivery," as the fourth intellectual art. He divided this art or "kind of rational knowledge" into the "organ," the "method," and the "illustration of tradition." Speaking of "method," Bacon declared with reference to Ramus, "I see it hath moved a controversy in our time."[13] Central to this controversy were questions about the relative merits of various types of method. Ramus had identified two major categories of method, "natural" and "cryptic or hidden." That Ramus's strongly proclaimed preference for natural method was well respected by his followers is indicated by the fact that in the first English translation of Ramus's *Dialectic*, Roland MacIllmaine nearly omitted his treatment of cryptic method.

Disagreements about method in the rhetorical tradition during the sixteenth and seventeenth centuries were primarily concerned with composition of oral and written discourse, but Ramus's comments about method made it clear that attempts to establish a theory and pedagogy of reading could not ignore disputes about method. Ramus had applied natural method to reading in his description of the process of unweaving a text:

> When you have cut out from the parts of the continuous discourse the many syllogisms therein, . . . take away all the amplifications, and, after making brief headings to note the arguments used, form into one syllogism the sum total of the discourse, this sum total being ordinarily self-evident, although it may be swelled to undue proportions by accumulation of ornaments.[14]

Bacon responded to the Ramistic tradition's limiting view of method by including method among the topics to be studied both specifically and generally in his new inquiry into communication. Bacon's study influenced the development of a "new rhetoric" in the latter half of the eighteenth century. Bacon's position was shared by later writers on the art of reading. He called for a return to, and an expansive exploration of, an ancient rhetorical principle, namely, that in the process of communication consideration of method must be subordinate to consideration of the writer's or speaker's purpose in relation to the audience addressed and the subject treated. As Karl Wallace observed:

> By Method [Bacon] meant primarily a way or technique of organizing and expressing subject matter according to the end sought and the audience addressed. . . . Some methods depend upon the type of subject-matter handled and upon the auditors, whether they be the speaker's critics or his pupils; other methods . . . are determined by the author's purpose, whether his discourse be designed to explain or to win consent.[15]

The hazards of a narrow view of method were clear to Bacon:

> . . . howsoever contention hath been moved touching a uniformity of method in multiformity of matter, yet we see how that opinion,

besides the weakness of it, hath been of ill desert towards learning, as that which taketh the way to reduce learning to certain empty and barren generalities; being but the very husks and shells of sciences, all the kernel being forced out and expulsed with the torture and press of the Method.[16]

Bacon offered examples showing the appropriate employment of multiform methods. He encouraged further examination of method, which he had judged to be, among his predecessors, "so weakly inquired as I shall report it deficient."[17] In his section on method in *The Advancement of Learning,* Bacon considered the need for inquiry into the varieties of method primarily from the point of view of the resources of writers or speakers. However, at the end of his section "Elocution, Tradition, or Delivery," Bacon pointed to the need for further inquiry into the resources of readers. Bacon declared:

There remain two appendices touching the tradition of knowledge, the one critical, the other pedantical. For all knowledge is either delivered by teachers, or attained by men's proper endeavours: and therefore as the principal part of tradition of knowledge concerneth chiefly writing of books, so the relative part thereof concerneth reading of books.[18]

Bacon's suggestion that a proper study of reading would require addressing issues pertaining to method was heeded by eighteenth-century writers on reading. Questions about uniformity versus multiplicity in methods were to be of major interest in eighteenth- and early nineteenth-century reading theory and pedagogy. Among the several questions pertaining to method that were discussed in eighteenth-century reading studies were those asking whether a uniform method for unweaving all texts was possible.

## DISAGREEMENTS ABOUT STYLE: RHETORIC AND THE STUDY OF READING

Many eighteenth-century writers on reading examined matters pertaining to rhetoric's second procedural canon, method or arrangement, in conjunction with exploring the third procedural canon, style. In the rhetorical tradition style or expression was concerned with fitting the proper language to the material discovered in the process of invention.

Traditional treatments of style, like those of method, presented writers on reading with competing conceptions.

Discussions of style inevitably involve assumptions about relationships between thought and language. Of crucial importance in all theory of communication are two competing conceptions of these relationships. One position presupposes that thought and language are strictly separable phenomena, often related only in an adversarial way. The opposing position assumes that there is some degree of interdependence, if not inseparability, between thought and language. The latter assumption informs the first stages of the rhetorical tradition; it is apparent as early as the pre-Socratic sophists who conceived of rhetoric as a study that developed both thought and expression at the same time. This view of a cooperative relationship underlay the classical conception of *ornatus,* which is often misunderstood. As Aldo Scaglione has noted, effective style consists of *ornatus:*

> not in the sense of a more or less gratuitous, artificial, and conventional adjunct to the plain, direct, "natural" expression, but in the sense of any expressive form that the effective use of language will necessarily assume. The insertion of some figures of speech into the grammar course was indicative of the fact that language and style, *langue* and *parole* if we may borrow a modern distinction, were, though rather vaguely, sensed as ultimately inseparable.[19]

The view that language and thought are closely linked appeared in works associated with the pedagogy of the new humanism. Erasmus's highly influential *De Copia,* for example, clearly treated figures as tools of *copia* that could expand or contract thought. Terence Cave has amply demonstrated that Erasmus's handling of the figures firmly rejected the status of figures as mere ornaments.[20] Erasmus believed that a properly organized study of the resources of language and of exemplary uses of those resources would provide education in the habits of thought necessary for effective expression in written or oral composition. Understanding the multiple resources of the language itself and exposure to examples of their use were, in Erasmus's view, means of training *thinking.*

The Erasmian view, of course, had to do with Latin composition and classical literature. Nonetheless, the idea that style and thinking are interrelated informed the early stages of the new humanism in England. It is not surprising, then, that as English literature and language came to be recognized as having a heritage of their own, a growing number of theorists and pedagogues began to apply the Erasmian point of view to their study of the "native tongue." George Williamson has shown in *The Senecan Amble* that through the sixteenth century in England, versions of the cooperative relationship between thought and the multiple resources of language occurred in Bacon's treatment of "the art of elocution," as well as in the works of Richard Sherry, George Puttenham, and John Hoskins, works which stand in the tradition of "stylistic rhetoric."[21]

Some manuals in the tradition, such as those of Sherry, Puttenham, and Hoskins, offered enlightening records of what Stanley Fish, agreeing with Morris Croll, refers to as " 'athletic movements of the mind by which it arrives at a sense of reality.' "[22] Some "stylistic rhetoricians," such as those I have mentioned, had aims similar to those of Erasmus in *De Copia*. They provided compilations of the customary methods of expanding thought and expression beyond the limits imposed by the habits of individuals in the day-to-day, conversational uses of the language. These manuals were designed to be records of forms of language used by speakers and writers on a wide variety of subjects and in a wide variety of circumstances.

The justification that Puttenham, for example, saw for collecting an extensive assortment of customary forms of thought and expression has been well described by Lawrence Manley: "Puttenham's theory suggests that poetic art achieves its ends . . . by drawing upon and manipulating such intellectual structures as have been previously established and sanctioned by custom."[23] As perpetuators of customary forms of *copia,* recorders of the methods employed by writers and speakers in order to vary thought and expression, these stylistic rhetoricians stood on the side of customary use in what became, in the seventeenth century, an increasingly intensified debate between those who stressed the resources of customary use and those who extolled the advantages of an idealized language or an idealized use of language.

The assumption that thought and the multiple resources of language are strictly separable underlay the firm and very influential Ramistic division between dialectic and rhetoric, with its assignment of invention and arrangement to dialectic, and of style and delivery to rhetoric. This division reduced figures and tropes to embellishments of already formulated thought. Reflections of belief in the decorative status of figures and tropes appeared in a number of highly respected sources. Thomas Sprat's well-known assault on metaphor in "scientific" writing reflected the assumption that thought is separable from such resources of language as figures and tropes. So, too, did Locke's later denunciation of rhetoric.

There has been a tradition of treating opposing views about style and pedagogy as representing a clash between advocates of Ciceronian style and those of plain style, but the clash was more subtle. When in 1967 Stanley Fish modified Morris Croll's pioneering discussions of anti-Ciceronianism, he provided a reminder that the conflict was more fundamental than earlier discussions had implied. Fish pointed out that the plain style associated with the "scientific movement" was not the plain style that Croll had identified with anti-Ciceronianism. Fish argued that the two styles "share an ideal-mirror-like fidelity to a reality. It is the realities that differ, at least in the early stages of each movement when goals are unambiguously stated."[24]

Fish underscored the general view that conceptions of style are often the products of radically conflicting assumptions about the operations of the mind and the roles language plays in those operations. This point is important because several eighteenth-century and early nineteenth-century writers on reading held differing views of style that were extensions of competing epistemological assumptions. Since competing theories of knowledge undergirded rival notions of style, fundamental issues divided those who viewed figures as ornaments and those who viewed figures as strategic instrumentalities.

Murray Cohen, in his examination of later eighteenth-century developments in English language theory, has identified a shift that suggests some of the epistemological struggles underlying competing conceptions of style. Cohen notes:

> Style, a century before, was the pattern of language appropriate to the subject of the discourse, a definition consistent with a view of language that stressed the correlation between language and things. Now [in the latter half of the eighteenth century], style is the pattern of language manifesting the speaker's attitude toward or understanding of his subject. This definition is consistent only with an approach to language that emphasizes the relationship between language and its users.[25]

Cohen's characterization of the shift in conceptions of style is valuable, but the view of style he associates largely with the latter half of the eighteenth century was actually asserted, in the study of reading, early in the century. Isaac Watts insisted that readers could ill afford to minimize authors' particular perceptions of their subjects, perceptions that would be manifest in an author's style.

Eighteenth-century writers on reading had a considerable stake in these disagreements about style, and their works provide a long-overlooked source for observing conflicting conceptions of style. Their differences also raised fundamental issues that any theory of reading must confront. It is of great practical importance whether one instructs a reader to attend to the subject of the discourse thus disregarding how the subject is written about, or whether one directs a reader to study carefully how each writer chooses to deal with his or her subject. Moreover, each kind of instruction implies a distinctive theory of meaning, as eighteenth- and nineteenth-century writers on reading discovered.

## DISAGREEMENTS ABOUT MEANING: GRAMMAR AND THE STUDY OF READING

The rhetorical tradition, with its rival conceptions of method and style, beckoned a number of students of reading. Grammatical studies, however, were particularly pertinent to answering the question, What relationships hold, or do not hold, between principles pertaining to oral reading and those pertaining to silent reading?

In *The Advancement of Learning,* Bacon divided grammar into "two natures": "the one popular, which is for the speedy and perfect attaining languages as well for intercourse of speech as for understanding of authors; the other philosophical, examining the power and nature of words, as they are the footsteps and prints of reason."[26] Both of these branches of grammar received attention from members of the Royal Society, but it was the philosophical branch that they found most important to their work of scientific reform. Their interest was primarily in language as a system of references. The desire to express "so many things almost in an equal number of words" generated extensive inquiry into "the power and nature of words."

The effort that marked the reformers' studies of language was largely an attempt to stabilize and promote versions of a referential theory of meaning. Whether it manifested itself as the construction of an ideal language or the "fixing" of a "natural" language, the object of the reformers was the promotion of a language that would clearly reflect "things." Focusing their attention on individual units of language (words, signs), many of the reformers envisioned the possibility of an ideal transparency in which each word could be a clear representation of a thing. This line of inquiry implied that, as William Alston writes:

every meaningful expression names something or other, or at least stands to something or other in a relation something like naming (designating, labeling, referring to, etc.) . . . The supposition is that for any meaningful expression, we can understand what it is for it to have a certain meaning by noting that there is something or other to which it refers.[27]

As Alston later notes, "the referential theory of meaning is based on the fundamental insight that language is used to talk about things."[28] For the interests of many of the Gresham reformers we need only change "is" to "can be."

The most influential concept of meaning to grow out of work associated with Royal Society reform was that outlined by John Locke in his discussion of words in the *Essay Concerning Human Understanding*. It has long been recognized that the enormous impact of Locke's theory of meaning resulted less from its originality than from its conjunction with a theory of knowledge in the *Essay*.[29] Locke's view of meaning bears the marks of the Gresham reformers' crusade against the abuse of words. Locke, like his Royal Society compatriots, concentrated attention on the individual units of language (words) and their capacities for representation.

In keeping with his speculations about "ideas," Locke shifted the primary focus of study from the word-thing relation to the word-idea relation. He explored what is sometimes referred to as an ideational theory of meaning, which holds that a word or expression comes to have a particular meaning by being used repeatedly as the mark of a certain idea.[30] The Lockean version of an ideational theory posited ideas with which the mind operates but which are fully independent of language. Alston suggests, the rudiments of an ideational theory had received attention long before Locke's writing. "This kind of theory," Alston writes, "is in the background whenever people think of language as a 'means or instrument for the communication of thought,' or as a 'physical and external representation of an internal state,' or when people define a sentence as a 'chain of words expressing a complete thought.' "[31] The new, and soon to be controversial, life that Locke brought to previous thinking lay in his epistemology's stress on clear, distinct, individual ideas, fully isolable from mere words.

Locke's theory of ideas and attention to word-idea relations posed no threat to his predecessors' concentration on word-thing relations. He provided what he considered to be the essential epistemological assurance that all ideas ultimately derive from experience through sensation and reflection. Locke's route through ideas was more circuitous than that offered by his predecessors' word-thing model, but Locke argued that, with reductive effort, clear and distinct ideas of things can be signified in clear and distinct words.

Locke's view of meaning did not go unchallenged. One significant modification of Locke's view of meaning was grounded in the "common sensory" defense of the irreducibility of abstract ideas, a notion which was germane to a concept of meaning underlying the early development of the study of reading. Another challenge to Locke's theory of ideas, one strongly concerned with "common sense," was of consequence to later developments in reading.

The competing conceptions of style are integrally related to the referential and the ideational views of meaning. The conception of style as the pattern of language appropriate to the subject of the discourse implies that language and the phenomena of the world constituting the subject of discourse are *directly* related. The conception of style as the pattern of language that displays the writer's or speaker's attitudes toward and understanding of the subject is similar to the ideational view of meaning, in that it highlights the relation between language and the author's *conception* of the subject.

Conflicts between referential and ideational views of meaning gave rise to some of the disputes among eighteenth-century writers on reading. For example, the simplest forms of both referential and ideational views presuppose that the individual word is the basic unit of meaning. That assumption came to be doubted, then modified, and finally rejected by various students of reading. Eighteenth- and early nineteenth-century writers on reading became interested in what happens to the meanings of individual words when those words are joined in discourse, and they proposed four distinct models of contextual meaning, which I have called *key-word, utterance, sentence,* and *instrumental.*

Exploring contextual meaning in turn raised questions about how narrowly or broadly "context" was to be construed. Is a reader's search for meaning restricted to the words joined in the text? Is meaning partly a result of something that the text leaves unsaid and that must be supplied by the reader? Such questions forced students of reading to consider fundamental aspects of Bacon's "philosophical grammar," just as the same questions do to reading theorists today.

## FROM GRAMMAR TO SYNTAX

In addition to being influenced by seventeenth-century examinations of "the power and nature of words," eighteenth- and early nineteenth-century writers on reading were affected by explorations of what Bacon had identified as the second "nature" of grammar, the "popular, which is for the speedy and perfect attaining languages as well as for intercourse of speech as for understanding of authors."

The major such examination associated with the Royal Society was John Wallis's *Grammar of the English Tongue*. Wallis proposed to follow "a completely new method, which has its basis not, as is customary, in the structure of the Latin language but in the characteristic structure of our own."[32] While Wallis's claims for originality exceeded his accomplishment, his attempt to describe the characteristic structure of English influenced the development of a "new English grammar" tradition devoted to articulating the principles of the native tongue. By 1711–1712, the years in which three important and highly popular English grammars appeared, competition among the new grammars was sufficient to warrant publication of a volume reviewing English grammars, *Bellum Grammaticale*.[33] The three grammars reviewed were, James Greenwood's *Practical English Grammar* (1711), John Brightland and Charles Gildon's *Grammar* (1711), and Michael Maittaire's *English Grammar* (1712).[34]

These new English grammars recognized that there was a large audience for rudimentary training in writing and reading English. To meet the public demand, the manuals advertised themselves as general introductions for those who wanted to become skilled in basic principles of the native tongue. Diligent students, the manuals suggested, would develop extensive oral and written communication skills. The range of instruction they offered clearly represented an impulse to move textbooks and students beyond a consideration of individual words and their elements to a study of larger units of discourse. Yet recognition of the need to deal with such larger units preceded the grammarians' abilities to cope with the need, and the popular textbooks continued to embody the dominant post-Lockean concentration on the individual word, the part of speech, as the unit of meaning.

All of the grammars reviewed in the *Bellum Grammaticale* recognized the need to extend study of the native tongue to words joined together, and all professed an interest in matters of syntax. However, Brightland and Gildon, and Greenwood, forthrightly acknowledged an inability to guide students adequately beyond the study of individual words and articulated a need for supplementing current understanding of "the province of grammar."

At the end of their grammar, Brightland and Gildon added a short discourse on the sentence. They observed:

This is sufficient to give a full Idea of the Nature and Beauties of a Period, which I have inserted merely in compliance with Custom, being sensible that the Learner will be so far from being able to make his Advantage from it till he has arriv'd much beyond the Province of Grammar, but that there will be few Masters found, who have the Education of Children, who know anything of this Matter.[35]

This view that the province of grammar did not include matters relating to consecutive discourse was not confined to Brightland and Gildon. Greenwood, in *Practical English Grammar,* noted the need for a new kind of book to supplement the manuals on grammar. He said such a book "ought to contain not only single *Syllables* and *Words,* but *Sentences* and *Stories,*" and he believed that kind of work should call students' attention to "the coherence or agreement of the Parts of the Sentence."[36]

Greenwood's call for a supplement to grammar contributed directly to the development of studies of reading in the eighteenth century. Isaac Watts, in the first manual to employ the term "art of reading" in its title, spoke of Greenwood's reference to the need for supplementation. Watts presented his textbook as a partial answer to that need. Two points stand out about this new development: first, the treatment of reading as an art began with Watts, and second, the treatment of sentences and larger units of discourse was not thought of as a grammatical treatment.

The conception of reading as a study supplementary to grammar was prominent throughout the eighteenth and early nineteenth centuries. This implied one kind of answer to the master question, To what established intellectual enterprises should one turn to borrow principles for an independent study of reading? Several believed that an art of reading must borrow principles from grammar, but that supplementary theory must go on to refine and extend grammatical principles by exploring "words joined." This did not mean that art-of-reading studies should borrow only from grammar. For a number of writers, the argument that reading was supplementary to grammar reflected their sense that the study of reading needed also to draw on rhetorical principles. The resulting hybrid was sometimes called "rhetorical grammar," and this notion of combining grammatical with rhetorical principles is important to an understanding of eighteenth-century theory and pedagogy of reading.

In drawing on principles of grammar and trying to supplement them, reading theorists were forced to confront a dispute inherited from the grammarians. The disputed question was whether "spoken language" or "written language" was the primary form of linguistic communication.

The grammars of Greenwood and of Brightland and Gildon disagreed on this point, presenting rival views on which form of language should be of primary concern in education. Noting that the art of writing "is an Accident of Speech," Greenwood followed the dominant tradition by emphasizing speaking: "*Grammar* is the Art of Speaking rightly." Brightland and Gildon's grammar took issue with Greenwood's definition and said that the study of grammar "is of more Consequence In Writing" than in speaking.

During the first stage of the study of reading, writers attempted to achieve a difficult balance between attention to the spoken language and study of the written language. The new reading textbooks treated basic reading as primarily an oral activity with roots in the grammarian's traditional interests in the spoken language. However, writers of the new manuals also recognized that the fundamentals of reading dealt with problems related to how readers derive meaning from words joined in written or printed language, and so they gave attention to the capacities of the written language for conveying meaning.

Near the middle of the eighteenth century, proponents of the oral tradition reacted to what they perceived as neglect of the study of spoken language in the earlier part of the century. They dramatically argued that the study of spoken language had priority not only in grammatical inquiries but in more advanced language studies, particularly the study of reading. They charged that the written language was a feeble medium of communication and contrasted the limitations of writing in communicating intentions with the fuller capacities of speech. They stressed, as Cohen has noted, that intentions were most clearly conveyed "by techniques of oral delivery, by the effects of pitch patterns and intonation."[37] This reaction forced several writers on reading to address directly the master questions about meaning. The claims against the written language made it necessary to consider how authorial meaning is conveyed, whose meaning a reader discovers, and whose meaning an oral reader delivers to listeners.

Eighteenth-century debates about the relative merits of spoken and written forms of language uncovered several thorny issues that still concern current reading theory. The eighteenth and early nineteenth centuries produced a skepticism about textual stability that was as radical as any in the twentieth century. Among the various views of readers' activities were conceptions of readers as important contributors to the meanings of the work read. There were even views that nearly characterized the reader as the "writer" of the work read.

The struggle of eighteenth- and early nineteenth-century theorists to come to terms with relationships between spoken and written forms of language revealed itself in several ways, including shifts in the meanings of crucial terms employed by writers on reading. One of these terms, "emphasis," played such a prominent role that it deserves special attention. Its multiple meanings suggest the general questions about relationships between the spoken and the written forms of language.

One traditional view of emphasis classified the term among rhetorical figures. Emphasis often does function as a rhetorical figure in both written and spoken modes of language. In both forms the figure suggests something beyond that which is stated. In the seventeenth century, John Smith provided the following definition of emphasis in *The Mystery of Rhetoric Unveiled* (1657): "*Emphasis* is a figure whereby a tacite vertue and efficacy of signification is given unto words; Or it is a form of speech which signifieth that which it doth not expresse; the signification whereof is understood either by the manner of pronunciation, or by the nature of the words themselves."[38] Puttenham, in *The Art of English Poesie* (1589), included in his treatment of figures the notion that emphasis implies more than the language states, but he abandoned consideration of the figure in terms of manner of pronunciation and limited his discussion to choice of diction: "And one notable meane to affect the minde, is to inforce the sence of any thing by a word of more than ordinary efficacie, and nevertheles is not apparant, but as it were, secretly implyed."[39]

A more limited and specialized sense of emphasis appeared during the eighteenth century, when an active linguistic interest in detailed descriptions of language as used by speakers in ordinary discourse gave rise to a restricted use of the term. In that restricted eighteenth-century usage, emphasis was associated with the spoken language and was treated as a type of stress placed by a speaker on a part of a word, or on a word or words, for the sake of offsetting some part or parts of utterance from other parts. This raised the questions, what is the unit of stress and how is stress effected?

The sense of emphasis that refers to both the written and the spoken forms of language is the "rhetorical sense" of the term. The other, more limited concern with emphasis in the spoken form of language is the "linguistic sense." Both the rhetorical and linguistic senses of emphasis imply that the process of offsetting, underscoring, or stressing certain elements of discourse is an aid to the audience (reader or hearer). In the eighteenth century those who used the term in both of its senses also allowed for non-essential, "decorative" employments of emphasis, but their basic interest was in how emphasis assisted an audience to come to terms with the meanings of discourse. Consequently, writers on reading intertwined discussions of devices of emphasis with discussions of how meaning is conveyed.

Near the middle of the eighteenth century, these rival conceptions of emphasis created major difficulties for writers on reading. The logic of those who adhered to the limited, linguistic sense of emphasis moved them toward denying that emphasis was really possible in the written language. This implicit or explicit denial led other writers to undertake new explorations of rhetorical emphasis and to develop new ideas concerning how the written form of language conveyed authorial meaning. Later in the century, certain writers turned to rhetorical grammar and began to study English syntax more intensely than had been done before. The late eighteenth-century theorists interested in syntax came to see two rhetorical figures, antithesis and ellipsis, as specially representing *joined* grammatical and rhetorical functions in communication. In consequence rhetorical emphasis began to displace linguistic emphasis as the foundation of theory of reading. This move was not original, of course. The impulse to mingle grammatical and rhetorical concerns in the study of syntax was as ancient as the studies of grammar and rhetoric. As Aldo Scaglione has observed:

> The antithesis as a basic device for structural balance may well have been the earliest invention of rhetorical practice. . . . When the full-fledged periodic style came to fruition, we recognize the antithesis (which Quintilian latinized as *contrapositio*) as really a conspicuous case of a basic law underlying the dynamics of the period: the "cola" or constituent parts of the period are interrelated by an inner tension in which the form can reflect the contrast between the contents, the language can mirror the thought.[40]

During the Renaissance, Sanctius's *Minerva,* and the work of Despauterius and Linacer, among others, promoted study of interdependent grammatical and rhetorical interests in the study of syntax. Scaglione notes that Despauterius and Linacer transmitted

> two capital notions destined to exert a far-reaching impact on future elaborations: the assimilation of rhetorical areas into grammar under the heading of *syntaxis figurata;* and the theory of ellipsis, as part of the *figurata* and as principal explanation of all phenomena not immediately reducible to application of the basic, normal patterns.[41]

29

At the beginning of the eighteenth century, English grammarians recognized the need for study of English syntax, but they provided only very brief discussions of the topic. Some of those brief discussions, however, expressed the Renaissance impulse to view the interrelation of grammatical and rhetorical concerns in studying syntax. Short references to ellipsis, particularly in the study of English syntax, appeared in the previously mentioned new grammars. Greenwood commented on the importance of the "Doctrine of Ellipsis or Suppression of Words" and referred the inquiring reader directly to Sanctius's *Minerva*.[42] Brightland and Gildon held in their brief treatment of syntax that ellipsis was a necessary consideration, as did Maittaire in his grammar of 1712. The interest shown by these grammarians reemerged in later eighteenth-century reading theory and pedagogy.

The late eighteenth-century interest in relationships between rhetorical and grammatical functions within syntax was the precursor of a similar interest by present-day thinkers about reading. Geoffrey Hartman, for example, sees promising signs for the fate of reading in the work of "those who are presently expanding and rationalizing the historical study of rhetoric in the hope of evolving a scientific 'grammar' on the level of poetics."[43] Twentieth-century interest in the interrelated force of rhetorical and grammatical features of discourse is usually traced to the pioneering work of Roman Jakobson on aphasia. Jakobson handled the similarity disorder and the contiguity disorder by reference to two fundamental rhetorical figures: metaphor and metonymy. He linked metaphor and metonymy with Ferdinand de Saussure's associative "vertical" plane of language versus the syntagmatic "horizontal" plane, thereby producing a model that has been widely influential and controversial. Among those who have developed implications of the model toward a theory of reading is Tzvetan Todorov.

Controversies whose origins lie in the eighteenth century still continue. For example, Paul de Man in *Allegories of Reading* observes: "One of the most striking characteristics of literary semiology as it is practiced today, in France and elsewhere, is the use of grammatical (especially syntactical) structures conjointly with rhetorical structures, without apparent awareness of a possible discrepancy between them."[44] De Man faults Roland Barthes, Gérard Genette, Algirdas-Julien Greimas, and Todorov for "letting grammar and rhetoric function in perfect continuity, and in passing from grammatical to rhetorical structures without difficulty of interruption." However, de Man notes, the problem of distinguishing "the epistemology of grammar from the epistemology of rhetoric is a redoubtable task."[45] This caution of de Man's shows how important it is to attend to eighteenth- and early nineteenth-century writers who took on the "redoubtable task."

There is one further manifestation of Jakobson's model that bears on eighteenth-century thought about reading. As I suggested in discussing meaning and grammar, the search for some sort of stability in textual meaning was a central problem for eighteenth-century writers on reading. The later eighteenth-century turn to an exploration of relationships between rhetorical and grammatical concerns in the study of syntax was in part an attempt to locate a point of stability for a theory of reading. If we pursue the implications of Jakobson's model we find that, in the words of Terence Hawkes, " 'meaning' . . . according to Jakobson's account is not a stable, predetermined entity which passes, untrammeled, from sender to receiver."[46] In the various eighteenth- and early nineteenth-century searches for stability in textual meaning, we find several intriguing and forward-looking insights into the multiple problems of contextual meaning.

## BIBLICAL INTERPRETATION AND THE STUDY OF READING

There remains to be acknowledged another intellectual enterprise to which some writers turned to borrow principles for an independent study of reading. In Western cultures the secular study of reading has deep-seated links with developments in the history of biblical interpretation. The beginning of the eighteenth century was a particularly rich period in the history of biblical interpretation as it relates to secular reading. Several eighteenth-century writers on reading, some well schooled in principles of biblical interpretation, found it expedient to adapt basic concerns of biblical interpretation. They addressed longstanding controversies in biblical interpretation, and in so doing they generated new insights for readers of secular texts.

Chief among the controversies about biblical interpretation were disagreements about the extent to which the language of a biblical text contains fully the meaning to be conveyed and the extent to which determination of meaning is subject to grammatical and philological analysis. At the beginning of the eighteenth century there were many responses to these questions, two of which were extreme versions of "enthusiastic" or highly intuitionist views of biblical interpretation, and arguments that a biblical text should be read like any other book. Characteristic of the first view was the belief that the biblical text initiates a spiritual communication far greater than, and not reducible to, the socially agreed-upon meanings of merely human language. Extreme enthusiastic views of biblical interpretation distrusted and discredited grammatical and philological analysis. Enthusiasts relied instead on the "inner light" of the faithful interpreter. The second view placed great stress on the humanness of the biblical writers and their location in particular historical circumstances, and it accepted tools of grammatical and philological analysis as valuable aids in the interpretive process.

Between the two extremes lay a host of moderate positions that defended the belief that the Bible was a book apart from other books while asserting that grammar and philology provided essential tools for the biblical interpreter. An important principle maintained by Erasmus, generally recognized as a prominent force in the development of biblical textual criticism, was that the "spiritual sense" must always be interpreted in relation to the "grammatical sense," which one arrived at by full exercise of linguistic skills. A prominent moderate view of interpretation in the early eighteenth century was that associated with August Hermann Francke of Halle and with a scholarly branch of pietism. Francke, whose works were known in England and who knew of the work of Isaac Watts, found the tools of grammar and philology to be essential aids in biblical interpretation. But Francke resisted a totally grammatical and philological approach to the the scriptures by holding to the notion that the biblical text conveyed "a spiritual sense above the ordinary grammatical and logical senses in at least some of the sacred words." This spiritual sense lent some words "an expanded force or emphasis."[47]

Eighteenth-century writers found biblical interpretation to be a significant source for models of the process of reading, but they also recognized it as a source infused with theoretical controversies. As those controversies became manifest in the secular study of reading, they helped to generate divergent strains of eighteenth-century theory concerning secular reading. Early in the century elements of enthusiastic biblical interpretation informed one line of thought about secular reading, while more moderate theories of interpretation informed another. Enthusiastic interpretation implied a notion of the limited powers of words *per se,* and by mid-century this idea had led some writers to charge that writing was an enfeebled medium of communication. That charge set other students of reading to exploring the nature of syntax. Thus it is fair to say that throughout the eighteenth century, influences of biblical interpretation can be seen identifying and shaping the issues that had to be faced in evolving a theory of secular reading.

All of these issues were raised in the work of two pioneers in reading theory and pedagogy, Isaac Watts and John Dennis, who offered divergent responses to these issues. In particular, they presented competing conceptions of style and operated from disparate epistemological assumptions. Chapter 2 is an analysis of their positions concerning the practice of secular reading.

NOTES TO CHAPTER 1

1. W. H. G. Armytage, *Four Hundred Years of English Education* (Cambridge: Cambridge University Press, 1964), p. 48.
2. M. G. Jones, *The Charity School Movement* (Cambridge: Cambridge University Press, 1938), pp. 18–19.
3. Jones, *Charity,* pp. 78–79.
4. Jones, *Charity,* p. 83.
5. Jones, *Charity,* p. 84.
6. Foster Watson, *English Grammar Schools to 1660* (Cambridge: Cambridge University Press, 1908), p. 173.
7. Watson, *English,* p. 176.
8. Irene Parker, *Dissenting Academies in England* (Cambridge: Cambridge University Press, 1914), p. 61.
9. Bonamy Dobree, *English Literature in the Early Eighteenth Century, 1700–1740* (Oxford: Oxford University Press, 1959), p. 334.
10. René Wellek, *Concepts of Criticism* (New Haven, Conn.: Yale University Press, 1963), p. 23.
11. Joseph M. Levine, "Ancients and Moderns Reconsidered," *Eighteenth-Century Studies* 15, no.1 (Fall 1981): pp. 82ff.
12. Wellek, *Concepts,* p. 28.
13. Francis Bacon, *The Advancement of Learning,* ed. G. W. Kitchin (1605; London: J. M. Dent, 1915), p. 140.
14. Walter Ong, *Ramus, Method and the Decay of Dialogue* (Cambridge: Harvard University Press, 1958), p. 191.
15. Karl R. Wallace, "Bacon's Conception of Rhetoric," in *Historical Studies of Rhetoric and Rhetoricians,* ed. Raymond F. Howes (Ithaca, N.Y.: Cornell University Press, 1961), p. 121.
16. Bacon, *Advancement,* p. 143.
17. Bacon, *Advancement,* p. 140.
18. Bacon, *Advancement,* p. 150.
19. Aldo Scaglione, *The Classical Theory of Composition* (Chapel Hill: University of North Carolina Press, 1972), p. 13.
20. Terence Cave, *The Cornucopian Text* (Oxford: Oxford University Press, 1979), pp. 3–34.
21. George Williamson, *The Senecan Amble* (Chicago: University of Chicago Press, 1951), pp. 163–64.
22. Stanley Fish, *Surprised by Sin* (London: Macmillan, 1967), pp. 124–25.
23. Lawrence Manley, *Convention* (Cambridge: Harvard University Press, 1980), p. 188.
24. Fish, *Sin,* pp. 124–25.
25. Murray Cohen, *Sensible Words: Linguistic Practice in England, 1640–1785* (Baltimore, Md.: The Johns Hopkins University Press, 1974), p. 103.

26. Bacon, *Advancement,* p. 138.

27. William Alston, *Philosophy of Language* (Englewood Cliffs, N.J.: Prentice Hall, 1964), p. 12.

28. Alston, *Language,* p. 19.

29. Norman Kretzmann, "History of Semantics," in *The Encyclopedia of Philosophy,* ed. Paul Edwards, (New York: Macmillan, 1967), vol. 7, p. 379.

30. Alston, *Language,* p. 23.

31. Alston, *Language,* p. 23.

32. John Wallis, *Grammar of the English Tongue,* ed. and trans. J. A. Kemp (1765; facsimile of 6th ed., London: Longman, 1972), p. 111. Wallis originally published the work in Latin under the title *Grammatica Linguae Anglicane.*

33. Generally attributed to Charles Gildon.

34. James Greenwood, *An Essay Towards a Practical English Grammar* (1711; reprint, Menston, England: The Scolar Press, 1968); Charles Gildon and John Brightland, *A Grammar of the English Tongue* (1711; reprint, Menston, England: The Scolar Press, 1967); Michael Maittaire, *The English Grammar* (1712; reprint, Menston, England: The Scolar Press, 1967).

35. Gildon and Brightland, *Grammar,* (1711; reprint), p. 147.

36. Greenwood, *Essay,* p. 232.

37. Cohen, *Words,* p. 107.

38. John Smith, *The Mystery of Rhetoric Unveiled* (1657; reprint, Menston, England: The Scolar Press, 1969), p. 256.

39. George Puttenham, *The Arte of English Poesie* (1589; reprint, Menston, England: The Scolar Press, 1968), p. 153.

40. Scaglione, *Composition,* p. 31.

41. Scaglione, *Composition,* p. 133.

42. Greenwood, *Essay,* p. 223.

43. Geoffrey H. Hartman, *The Fate of Reading* (Chicago: University of Chicago Press, 1975), p. 273.

44. Paul de Man, *Allegories of Reading* (New Haven, Conn.: Yale University Press, 1979), pp. 6–7.

45. de Man, *Allegories,* pp. 6–7.

46. Terence Hawkes, *Structuralism and Semiotics* (Berkeley: University of California Press, 1977), p. 84.

47. Hans Frei, *The Eclipse of the Biblical Narrative* (New Haven, Conn.: Yale University Press, 1974), pp. 38ff.

# 2

# THE KEYS TO UNDERSTANDING AND JUDGMENT:
## *The Alternative Reading Programs of Isaac Watts and John Dennis*

Although Isaac Watts and John Dennis are usually counted among the minor literary figures of their period, they made major contributions to the history of reading as well. Watts wrote on a wide variety of subjects ranging from logic to hymnology, and he had an intense interest in problems of education, which he approached by offering theoretical discussions of the current situation and needs of education and producing a few manuals or textbooks on particular subjects. In his various works he examined reading from several vantage points. In conjunction with outlining principles of understanding, some of his works treated principles of judgment in reading, or critical reading. In other works he dealt primarily with problems of basic literacy. His concern for literacy led him to write the first eighteenth-century "art-of-reading" textbook. The fact that Watts produced no single work devoted to the principles of critical reading is suggestive of his view of the relationships between the principles of reading for basic literacy and the principles pertaining to critical reading. For Watts, basic reading and critical reading were ultimately intertwined processes.

Watts was the initiator of an art-of-reading tradition that attempted to revive and adapt reading to a classical model for rhetorical training. Fundamental to the classical model was a unified view of training in the verbal arts: instruction in the principles and skills of comprehension and of judgment was conceived as a two-faceted but single enterprise.

John Dennis set himself a more limited task than did Watts. He was intent upon articulating principles of judgment, or principles of critical reading. Such activity he portrayed as quite distinct from acts of reading for understanding. Dennis was an early spokesman for attempts to set out principles of critical reading and "polite learning."

Watts maintained the highly catholic view that many disciplines, including logic, rhetoric, grammar, and biblical interpretation, contained principles that could profitably be appropriated in the study of reading. Dennis, however, focused attention primarily on principles of rhetoric and biblical interpretation. The enterprises to which they chose to turn, the principles they selected, and the ways in which they handled those principles reflected Watts's and Dennis's disparate epistemologies. In turn, the epistemological assumptions of each reveal their divergent answers to the master questions about meaning.

A major premise on which Watts and Dennis did agree was that the dominant Lockean epistemological model, which held that the rational capacities of the mind could be isolated and scrutinized, left serious problems unsolved. They also did not quarrel about the premise that an overly reductive concept of communication that had allied itself with the dominant Lockean epistemological model had resulted in a hazardous neglect of several forms of discourse. The reductive concept of communication against which Watts and Dennis reacted prized rational discourse and was intolerant of emotional appeals and forms of language associated with such appeals. In setting forward their own theories of communication, Watts and Dennis countered this dominant tradition. They resisted proposals by the Royal Society in the late seventeenth century for a strictly scientific mode of discourse. Sound communication, Watts and Dennis agreed, occurred in more complex and varied forms than strict rationalists perceived.

While Watts and Dennis agreed about these problems, they chose divergent courses in their search for solutions, and their choices of approaches to epistemological and communication problems were reflected in later reading studies. The primary distinction between their responses to the Lockean epistemological model can be discovered in what each did and did not concede to Locke's conceptions. Watts held that the Lockean model possessed many advantages, but he also discerned basic problems in its treatment of the fundamental operation of the faculty of the understanding. Dennis believed that the Lockean model adequately handled the faculty of understanding, but he claimed that there were other essential faculties or parts of mind whose importance was diminished, if not neglected, by the Lockean model. The different implications of these two objections to Lockean epistemology helped shape the debates about reading theory throughout the rest of the century.

36

Watts elaborated his agreements and disagreements with Locke in his widely influential *Logic,* which by 1728 was being used at both Oxford and Cambridge. It was later introduced at Yale, where it served as a textbook well into the nineteenth century. The work also became a major source of examples and definitions for Samuel Johnson's *Dictionary.*[1]

In *Logic* Watts postulated the "common sensory," a postulation that links *Logic* to several other eighteenth-century works, including writings of the later Scottish Common Sense Movement. Like the common sense theorists, Watts wanted to guard against forms of skepticism that he believed were encouraged, or at least allowed, by Locke's formulations. Watts supported Locke's concern for clarity in the relationship between words and the ideas for which they stand, and in *Logic* he offered no direct critique of Locke's assumption that individual words, as signs or marks of ideas, constitute the basic units of meaning. However, Watts did not agree with Locke's reduction of all ideas to their "springs" in sensation and reflection.

Watts contended that not all abstract ideas have their causes in ideas of sensation and reflection. According to Watts, some "arise from a power that is in the mind itself to abstract or divide one part of an idea from the other, or to separate mingled ideas and conceive them apart."[2] In "The Original of our Ideas," Watts summed up his epistemological departure from Locke:

> If therefore we confine ourselves strictly and entirely to those two things which Mr. Locke asserts to be the springs and causes of all our ideas, *viz.* sensation and reflection, without admitting this third principle, *viz.* the soul's power of comparing ideas and abstracting one from another, we shall hardly account for the numerous abstracted ideas which we have, whereof many are neither intellectual nor corporeal, though they are all evidently at first derived from corporeal or from spiritual objects and ideas; and the original remote springs of them may be sensation or reflection, though these are not the immediate causes of them.[3]

The "third principle" occupied a major position in Watts's *Logic.* He identified two sorts of ideas produced by that "act of the mind, which we usually call abstraction": absolute and relative. He noted that the first "are the most absolute, general, and universal conceptions of things considered in themselves, without respect to others, such as being, and not being, essence, existence, act, power, substance, mode, accident, &c."

The second sort he wrote, "is relative, as when we compare several things together, and consider merely the relations of one thing to another, entirely dropping the subject of those relations, whether they be corporeal or spiritual; such as our ideas of cause, effect, likeness, unlikeness."[4] Watts added that "most of the terms of art, in several sciences, may be ranked under this head of abstracted ideas, as noun, pronoun, verb, in grammar, and the several particles of speech as wherefore, therefore, when, how, although, howsoever, &c. so connections, transitions, similitudes, tropes, and their various forms in rhetoric."[5] In both *Logic* and "The Original of our Ideas," Watts separated ideas produced by the act of mind called abstraction from ideas of sensation and reflection, and he asserted that the immediate causes of the former were not to be found in the latter.

As is suggested in his comment about certain terms in relation to abstract ideas, Watts believed that epistemology must be brought into harmony with an adequate view of how language works. In his attempt to achieve this harmony Watts carried his quarrel with Locke from the realm of epistemology into the realm of communication. Locke's ideational theory of meaning, faithful to its epistemological base, held that in communication, reduction of meanings conveying abstract ideas is necessary. For Thomas Hobbes and some of Locke's Royal Society contemporaries, the forms of reduction were available in the definitional procedures associated with a philosophic or scientific use of language. Those definitional procedures were an important point of distinction between scientific and the far less rigorous, common uses of language. In keeping with his epistemological departure from Locke, Watts recognized that the reductive model was ill equipped to handle all ideas and all words that stand for them. An adequate conception of meaning required that the measures for achieving ultimate clarity in communication be more extensive than those prescribed by the reductive model and must even include and explain figures of rhetoric. Watts contended that several of the measures for achieving ultimate clarity in communication were to be found among the "common methods of speech."

Observing that "a multitude of . . . abstracted ideas belong to common speech," Watts contended that the common methods of speech provided a suitable medium for conveying irreducible abstract ideas.[6] He noted:

> Mr. Locke . . . supposes the communication of motion from one body to another by impulse to be as hard to be accounted for as the communication of motion to a body by any thoughts or volitions

of the mind. . . . And yet we still use the common methods of
speech, and say, that bowl A striking bowl B, naturally makes it
move.[7]

Watts added that we must indeed use such common methods of speech,
for

unless we continue to use such forms of expression, which are the
constant language of God and men in Scripture, and in all natural
and civil affairs, we shall almost destroy the very notion of cause
and effect among created beings . . . and . . . exclude all dependency
of created beings upon each other, and their several connections.[8]

Thus Watts stopped well short of the final reductive stages of the Lockean view of meaning, just as he did in reference to the last reductive
stages of Lockean epistemology.

The previously mentioned third principle of the soul, with its power of
abstraction and associated terms of art including the figures of rhetoric,
constituted an essential link between Watts's epistemology and his conception of meaning. In his conception of meaning the ornamental view
of rhetorical figures was set aside in favor of conceiving figures as strategic instrumentalities in the process of communication.

Watts's discussion of the meanings of words considered individually
paralleled his treatment of the "act of the mind which is called abstraction." In the act of abstraction there is

a withdrawing some part of an idea from other parts of it: For
when singular ideas are first let into the mind by sensation or reflection, then, in order to make them universal, we leave out, or
drop all those peculiar and determinate characters, qualities,
modes, or circumstances, which belong merely to any particular
individual being, and by which it differs from other beings; and we
only contemplate those properties of it, wherein it agrees with
other beings."[9]

One parallel to the mind's act of abstraction can be found in Watts's
ideas about the relationships between names and the ideas for which
they stand. Having emphasized that there is "no natural connection"
between words and "the ideas they are designed to signify" and that
"words and names . . . are merely arbitrary signs invented by men to
communicate their thoughts or ideas to one another," Watts took up in
*Logic* questions of relationships between words and ideas. In discussing

words in relation to complex ideas, he noted a fundamental principle of language in which single words are "invented to express complex ideas, in order to make language short and useful." This principle of economy introduces a form of abstraction in which the single word is made to stand for some property shared by the various simple ideas that constitute the complex idea. The principle of economy is invoked for the sake of pointing out "some chief property which belongs to the thing that the word signifies."[10]

Watts believed that a further parallel between the mind's act of abstraction and the structure of language existed in the manner in which language comes to accommodate new "inventions" and new ideas. In the act of abstraction, he argued, we aim at "those properties of [a being] wherein it agrees with other beings." This act of perceiving essential resemblances has its parallel in another principle of economy in language. Watts noted that "the world is fruitful in the invention of utensils of life, and new characters and offices of men, yet names entirely new are seldom invented; therefore old names are almost necessarily used to signify new things."[11] This process of transfer, as described by Watts, depends on a perception of resemblance between the old and the new, which allows the old name to accommodate the new. Thus, "when gunpowder was found out, the word powder, which before signified only dust, was made then to signify that mixture or composition of nitre, charcoal, &c."[12] Watts described such a process of transfer in these terms: "Words change their sense by figures and metaphors, which are derived from some real analogy or resemblance between several things; as when wings and flight are applied to riches, it signifies only that the owner may as easily lose them, as he would lose a bird who flew away with wings."[13]

The metaphors Watts employed in discussing well-constructed discourse reflected yet another parallel between the mind's act of abstraction and the realm of language. During his discussion of illustrating or arguing a difficult point, Watts advised the student to "be not too scanty of words, but rather become a little copious and diffuse in your language: Set the truth before the reader in several lights, turn the various sides of it to view, in order to get a full idea and firm evidence of the proposition."[14] Discussing various sorts of discourse, Watts spoke of placing some aspects of a composition in a clear light while subordinating others to the shadows of the background, and elevating some aspects of the discourse while sinking others. The structure of the mind's act of abstraction is applied to the structure of discourse as a whole by metaphors such as these. For Watts, a good composition presents itself as a unified collectivity of simple and complex ideas, and the task of the writer is to display to the reader the essential characteristics of the structure of that unified idea, which Watts referred to as the "design" of the whole. A writer must amplify, condense, and vivify in order to facilitate the reader's contemplation of relationships or agreement among highlighted or heightened elements of a discourse. To use another familiar metaphor, the task is one of foregrounding some elements and backgrounding others.

In treating how sentences should be read, Watts took a *key-word* position. This position implied that figures and other terms are *strategically* implanted by authors in order to signal how the whole of a sentence is to be understood. In *The Art of Reading,* Watts directed readers to search sentences for words that seemed to be emphasized in the sentence. These emphatic words, he said, showed the "chief design" of sentences. They were put into the sentences in particular ways to indicate the author's intended meaning for the whole set of words. Watts expressed this notion of contextual meaning as follows: "For it is for the sake of that word, or words [which show the chief design], the whole sentence seems to be made."[15] Thus the reader is to search for the key word or words that unlock the meanings of individual sentences and of sentences in relation to one another.

As would be the case with many later studies, Watts's fundamental instruction for determining the meaning of words joined was most fully developed in his discussions of emphasis. In *The Art of Reading,* the chapter titled "Of Emphasis, or Accent which belongs to some special Word or Words in the Sentence" presents Watts's concerns with authorial design and with the notion that a writer best interprets himself. "The great and *general rule* to find out which is the emphatical word in a sentence, is this: *Consider what is the chief design of the speaker or writer;* and that word which shows the chief design of the sentence, is the *emphatical* word."[16]

The means by which writers assure that sentences properly display their key words for the contemplation of readers, Watts assured his readers, are found among the common methods of speech, and those methods include the figures of rhetoric. Watts's examples demonstrate that of the several resources available to writers, the structures of antithesis or opposition and the substructures of parallelism and symmetry were of greatest concern to him. For instance, Watts used this example of a sentence in which the key words are immediately apparent: "James is neither a *fool* nor a *wit,* a *blockhead,* nor a *poet.*" In Watts's view the two sets of overt oppositions (fool or wit, and blockhead or poet) direct the reader's attention primarily to the relation between the characteristics signified in each set. Only secondarily is attention focused on the possessor of these characteristics. The ideas signified in the overt oppositions are definitionally related to the ideas signified by other words in the sentence. The key ideas are elevated or brought into light through the structure of overt opposition.

Watts's example also illustrates the practical operation of his notion of abstraction. In discussing abstraction, Watts argued that contemplation is aided by the harmonious working of patterns of opposition and patterns of parallelism and symmetry. In abstraction, some properties of a complex idea are distinguished from others and attention is focused on the essential properties that are in agreement with or resemble other similarly isolated essential properties of ideas. Details or distinctions are subordinated as a person abstracts. In Watts's example the key words are highlighted not just by their opposition, but by patterns of parallelism and symmetry. As Watts said in "A Brief Scheme of Ontology": "All opposites placed near one another give a mutual illustration to each other, and make their distinct characters appear plainer. Hence proceeds the reason of foils among painters, and jewellers, orators and poets."[17]

Watts was suggesting some elements of a sophisticated theory and pedagogy of reading built on the foundation of a thorough study of figuration. However, at the point where one might hope that Watts would lead students of reading into a close examination of figuration, he fell silent. Such an examination was left to his successors. His original but incomplete analysis illustrated the complexity and uncertainty that characterized thinking about reading early in the eighteenth century.

Watts's view of the relationships between written and spoken forms of language, and his application of that view to the study of oral and silent reading, impeded his analysis of figuration. One of the master questions I have mentioned is, What relationships hold or do not hold between the written and the spoken forms of language? Watts did not see this question as very significant, and the reason can be traced to early eighteenth-century views of grammar. In Watts's treatment of reading there was relatively little that conflicted with what Thomas Sheridan would say at mid-century about the primacy of the spoken language. One reason for this was that Watts's manual reflected an ideal with which John Wallis began the new grammar tradition. As Murray Cohen points out, "Wallis argues throughout the *Grammatica* that the distinctive vocal features of English sounds are the bases of letters from which one can construct words, sentences and syntax."[18] In the early stages of the new grammar tradition "sounds, letters, and meaning" were treated as parallel systems of different elements of language. These elements were perceived as such by Watts, who downplayed distinctions between orality and literacy. By portraying movement from the oral to the written form of language as basically unproblematic, Watts also was reviving the classical model of rhetorical training, for use in education in reading, without acknowledging that any difficulties existed. For Watts there was not a tensive relationship between the oral dimensions of the classical model and those dimensions concerned with analysis of written language, as there would be for many of his successors in the art-of-reading tradition.

*The Art of Reading* provides two instances of presupposing an easy movement back and forth between words in print and words in utterance, and those two instances planted the seeds of a later controversy. The first is an injunction which echoed through eighteenth-century study of the art of reading:

> Let the tone and sound of your voice in *reading* be the same as it is in *speaking;* and do not affect to change that natural and easy sound wherewith you *speak,* for a strange, new, awkward tone, as some do when they begin to *read:* which would almost persuade our ears that the *speaker* and the *reader* were two different persons, if our eyes did not tell us the contrary.[19]

Watts conceived this aural advice as simply an extension of his notion that to understand, one must attend to ordinary use of language, to the common methods of speech and forms of expression.

A second instance of Watts's ambiguity concerning written and spoken forms of language occurred in his discussion of emphasis. In discussing how a reader should search out key words in sentences, Watts was thinking about the *rhetorical* sense of emphasis. There he focused attention on the printed page as the source for discovering authorial intent. When he turned to treat the *importance* of emphasis, however, Watts shifted his attention to the *aural* dimensions of emphasis, using the *linguistic* sense of the term. He wrote:

> To make it appear of how great importance it is to place the *emphasis* aright, let us consider, that the very sense and meaning of a sentence is oftentimes very different, according as the *accent* or *emphasis* is laid upon different words; and the particular design of the speaker is distinguished hereby, as in this short question, *May a man walk in at the door now?* If the *emphasis* be laid upon the word *man,* the proper negative answer to it is, *No but a boy may.* If

43

the *emphasis* be laid upon the word *walk,* the answer is, *No, but he may creep in.*[20]

Watts's shift in treating emphasis reflected a theoretical and expositional problem that would trouble study of reading for many years, namely, what was the relation of oral to written language? In dealing with discovery of authorial design, Watts considered how terms used in printed language display a writer's intention to make them "key" and therefore emphatic. Yet in order to illustrate how to get emphasis right, he turned from authorial design to the powers of a speaker and of utterance to control meaning. His assumption of a basic symmetry between written and spoken forms of language allowed him to make this shift without being confused or confusing. The same assumption and resulting shift of focus also allowed him to neglect close scrutiny of figuration in writing, for in the end his attention was on forms of aural emphasis rather than on emphasis through strictly verbal patterns. This hid problems that in the later study of reading became serious issues of debate.

Cohen's informative discussion of eighteenth-century British language studies refers to a "strikingly new idea . . . consistent with the new linguistic assumption" of the period between 1740–1785: the "inclusion of a brief section proving the importance of emphasis by showing how the shifting of emphasis from one word to another in a sentence also changes the meaning."[21] However, the idea and some of the "linguistic assumptions" with which it is associated actually appeared in 1721, some twenty years before the date suggested by Cohen. Further, it is worth remembering that the new idea had its debut in the first British manual, that of Watts, devoted to the art of reading.

Later in the century this "strikingly new idea," along with Watts's advice to "let the tone and sound of your voice in reading be the same as it is in speaking," came under close scrutiny. These two guidelines contributed to an important series of debates about the locus of contextual meaning that were carried out by later writers who attempted to intensify interest in the power of the spoken language.

Although Watts's theory and pedagogy of reading neglected an examination of the written form of language at a crucial point, it is important to bear in mind the interpretations that Watts set in motion for followers and opponents. Watts's view of how language works grew out of his modification of Lockean epistemology. His postulation of the mind's act of abstraction had its parallel in his key-word view of contextual meaning. If we take a whole sentence to be an idea made up of constituent ideas, the well-constructed sentence should display its meaning in a manner suggested by Watts's descriptions of the act of abstraction. The sentence should abstract or divide one part of an idea from the others, separate mingled ideas, and set some idea or ideas (key words) apart so that the reader can contemplate relationships between highlighted ideas of one sentence and those of another in the discourse.

The means by which writers can assure, through rhetorical emphasis, that their sentences properly display their key words are to be found, Watts assured his readers, among the common methods of speech, including figures of rhetoric. That Watts chose to concentrate on antithetical structures in his treatment of how rhetorical emphasis is displayed is illustrative of how he considered patterns traditionally described as rhetorical figures to be among the essential tools of communication.

Clearly the crux of Watts's disagreement with Locke over the status of the common methods of speech lay in the resemblance Watts found between the structure of the act of abstraction and those structures of language through which language can be made to mirror thought. By including forms of rhetoric such as antithesis among the indispensable common methods of speech, Watts, in contrast to Locke, offered a redemptive view of rhetoric. In response to the master question, To which established intellectual enterprises should one turn to borrow principles and tools for an independent study of reading? Watts could comfortably have answered "rhetoric," as Locke could not.

Watts's redemptive view of rhetoric reflected a perception of rhetoric that runs counter to some prominent twentieth-century accounts of how rhetoric was construed in England in the sixteenth, seventeenth, and eighteenth centuries. One such prominent account occurs in Wilbur Samuel Howell's treatment of conceptions of style and elocution. Howell articulates a widely held view that the British rhetorical tradition's interest in figures and tropes from the sixteenth through the eighteenth centuries can be summed up largely as a concern with departures from ordinary ways of speaking, and with the accompanying notion that figures and tropes are decorations of plain thought or decorative alternatives to plain language. In his account of the early-eighteenth-century rhetorician John Ward, Howell observes:

> The notion that dignity of style is achieved when a pattern of verbal expression repudiates the patterns of ordinary speech and suits itself to the patterns of learning and politeness was fully worked out by Ciceronian rhetoricians of the sixteenth and seventeenth centuries in their elaborate and endless analysis of each one of several hundred tropes and figures.[22]

45

Howell's observations on a much earlier contribution to the British rhetorical tradition are similar. Of George Puttenham's treatment of figures and tropes under the heading of style, Howell writes:

> This view amounts to a denial that the language of ordinary life can be a medium for oratory or poetry. It also amounts to an affirmation that the medium for oratory and poetry can be found only by dressing up the language of ordinary life with such violations of our daily speech as the tropes and the figures represent.[23]

As an account of some assumptions (e.g. Ward's) about style in England in the sixteenth, seventeenth, and eighteenth centuries, Howell's observations are apt. However, there was an important countertrend in British conceptions of style, and without notice of this fact Howell's statements are misleading. Watts, far from conceiving of style as Howell describes, held views quite contrary to those Howell attributes to Puttenham. Indeed, Lawrence Manley disagrees with Howell even about Puttenham, saying Puttenham's observations indicate that "poetic art achieves its ends . . . by drawing upon and manipulating such intellectual structures as have been previously established and sanctioned by custom."[24]

Watts's epistemological response to Locke allowed him to see the rhetorical functions of figures. Furthermore, Watts claimed that the essential properties of certain rhetorical figures were properties of common methods of speech—methods he defended as necessary for communication between minds possessing the "third principle," the power of abstraction. To put the claim differently, rhetorical figures stand with the common methods of speech at the nexus of the basic operations of thought and the basic operations of language.

Paul de Man, in one of his recent discussions of the tropological nature of language and discourse, has argued that when Locke (who "would be the last man in the world to realize and to acknowledge this") "develops his own theory of words and language, what he constructs turns out to be in fact a theory of tropes." Further, de Man finds that Etienne Bonnot de Condillac, in his *Essai sur l'origine des connaissances humaines,* unintentionally provides an even "wider perspective on the tropological structure of discourse."[25] A subtheme in de Man's discussion is that Locke's account of words and their abuse blindly contained its own contradiction and so generated lines of thought among those who, like Condillac, considered themselves to be followers of Locke. A powerful form of such resistance to Locke's account of words can be seen in

46

Watts, who generally followed Locke. The deviation from Locke occurred in Watts's recognition that the structures and functions of figures are not reducible to the class of much-abused ornaments, decorations, or embellishments of thought. Other forms of loyal resistance to Locke arose among students of reading whom I discuss later.

Watts's revisionist conception of the rhetorical canon of style was linked to his reconsideration of the rhetorical canon of *dispositio,* arrangement, or method. Given his rejection of reductionist views of how words mean when they are joined, it was logical for Watts to argue against models of discourse that postulated ideal forms of arrangement dictated by subject matter. He cautioned writers against assuming such an ideal, and he warned against making such an assumption when reading. Watts claimed that various legitimate methods of arrangement are open to any writer on any subject. This position led him to advise readers to look for the particular "design" of a writer, as that design is manifested in the linguistic choices the writer has made.

Watts, speaking as a writer, said in his preface to *Horae Lyricae,* "I thought it lawful to take hold of any handle of the soul."[26] This comment reflects a concern that cut across several of Watts's treatises, including the preface, his work in hymnology and translation, "The Improvement of the Human Mind," and *Logic.* In all those works Watts resisted the tendency, exemplified in the Ramistic tradition, to attribute priority to a "natural" method of arranging discourse. In Watts's mind this narrow view of method lost sight of the many "handles of the soul."

Watts's definition of method in *Logic* was central to his conception of reading. There he said, "Method, taken in the largest sense, implies the placing of several things, or performing several operations, in such an order, as is most convenient to attain some end proposed."[27] He insisted that considerations of arrangement are subservient to particular "designs" or "proposed ends" that writers can have. Watts was intent upon dispelling any desire on the part of a reader to impose on a text prior expectations about an ideal method of arrangement. The same theme appeared in his examination "Of Study, or Mediation" in which he referred to a version of positivist reduction popular in the period. He said that under the influence

> derived from mathematical studies, some have been tempted to cast all their logical, their metaphysical, and their theological and moral learning into the method of mathematicians, and bring every thing relating to those abstracted, or those practical sciences under theorems, problems, postulates, scholiums, corollaries, &c.

whereas the matter ought always to direct the method; for all subjects, or matters of thought, cannot be moulded or subdued to one
form."[28]

Without denying an occasional usefulness of the natural method extolled
by the Ramistic tradition, Watts briefly discussed the analytic and syn-
thetic branches of natural method and appended a comment unsympa-
thetic to Ramism: "Upon the whole, I conclude that neither of these two
methods should be too scrupulously and superstitiously pursued, either
in the invention or in the communication of knowledge." Here he reiterated, "And indeed a wise and judicious prospect of our main end and
design must regulate all method whatsoever."[29]

After treating the natural method, Watts turned to "arbitrary method,"
which he defined as a method that "leaves the order of nature, and
accommodates itself to many purposes."[30] He reminded his readers that
"there are some subjects that can hardly be reduced to analysis or synthe-
sis," and he discussed arbitrary method in relation to "reading or writing
history," writing biography, and composing "poesy and oratory."[31] He
pointed out that there are advantages in arbitrary, cryptic, or hidden
methods. Those methods allow writers of these different sorts of discourse to "adapt everything to their designed ends." In *Logic* and other
works, Watts treated the multiple possibilities of arbitrary method with a
dignity appropriate to his concept of the many handles of the soul.

Watts is rarely thought of as a participant in the rhetorical tradition,
but his treatment of method in his extensively circulated *Logic* is highly
sensitive to central principles of rhetoric. As is suggested by his appreciation for the many handles of the soul, Watts accepted without reluctance
that audiences and their various circumstances are vital factors in determining what is, in the given case, the best process of communication.
Consideration of the audience informs Watts's repeated discussions of
the design of the author. Underscoring the importance of attending to
the multiplicity of methods, Watts advised writers to try "proportioning
the amplitude of your matter, and the fulness of your discourse to your
great design, to the length of your time, to the convenience, delight, and
profit of your hearers."[32] This is, without question, rhetorically oriented
advice.

Watts's concern with the role of the audience in the process of communication encouraged an approach to reading that stood in opposition to
the view of reading that assumed that a single reductive method could
unweave and be appropriate to all texts. His fundamental demand that

the reader consider the design of the author was a call to recognize that writers have available to them more than one legitimate form of arrangement for communicating and so will vary their methods with various audiences. This is why readers must entertain questions about the nature of the audience being addressed through the particular forms of arrangement chosen by the author.

Watt's defense of the common methods of speech, his acceptance of multiplicity of methods, and his acknowledgment that diverse audiences encourage diverse methods reflect an approach to reading that was more complex and required more versatility on the part of readers than the approach encouraged by Dennis and other contemporaries of Watts. The reader who accepted Watts's charge to relinquish allegiance to a single method for unweaving all texts faced the humbling recognition that authorial design can be signaled in diverse ways.

In addition to borrowing from rhetoric, Watts also borrowed from the tradition of biblical interpretation to flesh out his concepts of how one ought to read. In doing so, he had to take a position on the text-centered theory of interpretation embedded in the familiar hermeneutic principles, "Scripture is the best interpreter of Scripture" and "a writer best interprets himself." Watts's golden rule of reading did not deny these principles, but he certainly construed them more loosely than did some biblical interpreters. He advised readers to "treat every author, writer, or speaker, just as you yourselves would be willing to be treated by others, who are searching out the meaning of what you write or speak."[33] Watts's counsel gave considerable latitude to the reader as interpreter, even when reading sacred texts.

In *The Improvement of the Human Mind,* which was the supplement to *Logic,* the eighth chapter ("Of Enquiring Into the Sense and Meaning of the Writer or Speaker, and especially the Sense of the Sacred Writings") contains "rules" for "searching out the meaning" of what is read. In their bald forms the rules came from the tradition of biblical interpretation, but in Watts's hands they became rules for searching out the "scope and design" of either secular or sacred writers. Design rather than literal signification was Watts's key to all interpretation. His rules illustrate the basic view that authors use language *strategically* and do so either by habit or by design. For example: "Compare the words and phrases in one place of an author, with the same or kindred words and phrases used in other places of the same author, which are generally called parallel places." Intention, then meaning, are discovered by watching *usage.* Meanings are not ordained or fixed.

49

The same principle crops up in Watts's first two rules, which also reflect his conviction that common methods of speech and forms of customary usage are the basic resources used designedly by authors:

> I. Be well acquainted with the tongue itself, or language wherein the author's mind is expressed. Learn not only the true meaning of each word, but the sense which those words obtain when placed in such a particular situation and order. Acquaint yourself with the peculiar power and emphasis of the several modes of speech, and the various idioms of the tongue. . . .
> II. Consider the signification of those words and phrases, more especially in the same nation, or near the same age in which that writer lived, and in what sense they are used by authors of the same nation, opinion, sect, party, &c."[34]

What is important to notice about these rules and their like is that in their literal forms they unquestionably were derived directly from the tradition of biblical interpretation, yet for Watts they were procedures for discovering *purpose* and *strategy*, not linguistic signification *per se*.

Watts's modification of Lockean epistemology allowed him to see continuity and unity in the processes of comprehension and criticism. As I have noted, there were biblical interpreters who distrusted grammatical-philological approaches to texts. This distrust was particularly strong among those committed to "enthusiastic" pietism, who encouraged reading with guidance from an "inner light," a general view that eventually made its way into theories of secular reading. Watts, however, took a very different stand. As is implied in his rules for reading, Watts had a very broad view of "philological" knowledge and so found "philology" indispensable in reading texts. He also disagreed with those who believed that "style" had to do with special forms of speech. His epistemology, his belief in common methods of speech as the fundamental resources for communication, and his broad definition of philology led him to believe that there was no genuine distinction between reading for comprehension and reading critically. The latter process was simply a more intense application of the principles for reading for comprehension.

In the twentieth chapter of *The Improvement of the Mind* ("Of the Sciences and their Use in Particular Professions") Watts discussed what philological knowledge was needed for more than rudimentary reading of sacred or secular texts, and he alluded to contemporary controversies about the nature and place of "criticism." "The art of criticism is reckoned by some as a distinct part of philology," he said, but he continued, "History, grammar and languages, rhetoric and poesy" are all "included under the name of philological knowledge." With so broad a conception of philology, it was reasonable for Watts to assert that criticism

> is in truth nothing else than a more exact and accurate knowledge or skill in the other parts of it [philology], and a readiness to apply that knowledge upon all occasions, in order to judge well of what relates to these subjects, to explain what is obscure in the authors which we read, to supply what is defective, and amend what is erroneous in manuscripts or ancient copies, to correct the mistakes of authors and editors in the sense of the words, to reconcile the controversies of the learned, and by this means to spread a juster knowledge of these things among the inquisitive part of mankind.[35]

The position reflected Watts's view of how language works in discourse and his modifications of Locke's epistemology and concept of meaning. To Watts the various branches of philological knowledge collectively clarified meanings of both individual words and words joined in discourse. Philologically oriented reading was the exercise of an integrated set of activities that would produce useful understanding on which judgments could then be based.

Watts's views also make clear why he believed that aspects of classical rhetorical training could be adapted to the needs of eighteenth-century education in reading. The various tools of philology, properly conceived, opened the way to both understanding and criticism; hence a *full* address to the task and problems of reading was education in *both* comprehension and judgment—as classical theorists and pedagogues had maintained. Watts's insistence on broadly interpreting philology brings us back to his epistemological quarrel with Locke and the relationship between Watts's epistemology and his view of language.

Watts's notion that the various branches and tools of philology all provided paths toward the goals of understanding and judgment was based on his modification of Locke's model by injecting the idea of "common sensory" experience and on his related insistence that common methods of speech were the fundamental constituents of style. From these points of view, to isolate critical reading and assign it a privileged status relative to other philological functions was a mistake. So, too, was it a mistake to postulate an ideal, scientific language. Either move disregarded the "forms of expression" fundamental to "all natural and civil affairs," the common methods of speech.

Watts decided to compose his *Art of Reading and Writing English* for a number of reasons. He was prone to apply theoretical principles practically, and in this manual he distilled a number of his theoretical observations into a useful pedagogy. The manual was doubtless one of the works Samuel Johnson had in mind when he wrote (in reference to Watts) that anyone "acquainted with the common principles of human action, will look with veneration on the writer, who is at one time combating Locke, and at another time making a catechism for children in their fourth year."[36]

Watts's manual also made a point about the state of pedagogy, and it did so both explicitly and functionally. Watts said in his preface that existing textbooks did not carry students beyond the province of grammar into the larger province of reading. He was undertaking to remedy that oversight in a theoretically sound but practical way, although this was not a challenge to grammar *per se.*

Grammarians themselves had called for pedagogy that went beyond the limits of grammar narrowly defined. John Brightland and Charles Gildon, and James Greenwood, had written that books going beyond their own manuals were needed. The education of would-be readers required far more attention to words joined in discourse than grammar books gave such matters. In *The Art of Reading and Writing English,* Watts made clear that Greenwood's desire for a new kind of book motivated Watts to publish his manual. However, Watts said that his was only a limited attempt to supplement the study of grammar and that the full need could probably best be met by Greenwood. After directing his readers to Greenwood's grammar, "wherein he has shown the deep knowledge, without the haughty airs of a critic," Watts publicly urged Greenwood to publish an abstract of "the work he designs" to serve in "the instruction of common English readers."[37] Watts said in his preface that he had surveyed existing grammars and spelling books without finding the supplement to grammar that was called for, and he went on to propose something he had not attempted: an anthology of graded but varied reading. Such a collection, he thought, should move from "several easy portions of scripture . . . as well as other little composures" through "some well-chosen, short, and useful stories, that may entice the young learner to the pleasure of reading" to, "and the world will forgive me, . . . a few pieces of poesy."[38]

In *The Art of Reading* Watts expressed his beliefs that linguistic methods are multiform and that the fundamental elements of communication are the customary forms of speech. He also reiterated his contention that training in reading should prepare readers to handle a wide variety of designs and methods of fulfilling designs. Watts insisted that within the guidelines of customary usage there is a variety of "manners of writing" with which readers must become familiar. As to the purview of reading as a discipline or subject of study, Watts said that "reading in the most proper sense" begins at the level of words "joined together to make up sentences."

He continued by offering a clear, rhetorically oriented explanation of what reading "in the most proper sense" entailed:

> It is not so easy a matter to read well as most people imagine: There are multitudes who can read common words true, can speak every hard name exactly, and pronounce the single or the united syllables perfectly well; who yet are not capable of reading six lines together with their proper sound, and a graceful turn of voice, either to inform or to please the hearers; and if they ever attempt to read verse, even of the noblest composure, they perpetually affect to charm their own ears, as well as the company, with ill tones and cadences, with false accents, and a false harmony, to the utter ruin of the sense, and the disgrace of the poet."[39]

However, when Watts referred to managing the voice "according to the sense," he reflected his tendency to see no intellectual or pedagogical problems in moving thought and action from spoken to written forms of communication.

In his manual Watts offered only brief treatment of words joined together, but what he said was enough to show that he was trying to transform some of his more theoretical considerations of meaning and method into a reading pedagogy that emphasized contextual meaning. He repeated his key-word conception of contextual meaning and treated figures such as antithesis as strategic resources for communication. In his view, individual words in well-constructed sentences stand in interdependent, cooperative relationships in which the function of most words is to form the background against which key words or phrases are highlighted.

Watts's brief and simple textbook was the first in a line of English manuals on reading. It was a response to a recognized pedagogical need yet one that distilled sophisticated and systematic, though debatable and unfinished, work on the activity of reading. To see the full significance and design of Watts's thoughts about reading, one must read the manual in conjunction with such other of his works as *Logic*.

Watts's near-contemporary, John Dennis, addressed many of the problems treated by Watts; however, the solutions he advocated initiated a line of thought about reading radically divergent from that begun by Watts. Before Watts had sketched a theory and pedagogy of reading, Dennis had launched an exploration of aestheticism in British reading theory and pedagogy.

Dennis was primarily interested in articulating principles of critical reading, and so his work was carried out in the context of a debate about criticism that was part of an eighteenth-century "battle of the books." Some of the best-known assessment of the crisis of criticism in the early eighteenth century appeared in the work of Alexander Pope. While Pope directed several attacks at Dennis' practice of criticism, his lamentations about the general state of criticism in his day bore some resemblance to the complaints of Dennis. Pope translated his lamentations about the current state of criticism into instructions for critical readers. Fundamental to those instructions was a concern for discovery of authorial design, yet Pope's biting commentary on the faults and limitations of philology tended to undermine such ideas as Watts's image of a unified activity of reading.

A complaint by Pope in his commentary on criticism was that critics tended to focus on particular details in isolation, a failure that resulted from the critics' inability or disinclination to read for the author's design of the whole. In book 2 of the "Essay on Criticism" (1711) Pope provided the following directions:

> A perfect Judge will *read* each Work of Wit
> With the same Spirit that its Author *writ,*
> Survey the *Whole,* nor seek slight Faults to find,
> Where *Nature moves,* and *Rapture warms* the Mind . . .
>
> In Wit, as Nature, what affects our Hearts
> Is not th' Exactness of peculiar Parts;
> 'Tis not a *Lip,* or *Eye,* we Beauty call,
> But the joint Force and full *Result* of *all.*

Commenting on current critical practices, Pope wrote:

> Most Criticks, fond of some subservient Art,
> Still make the *Whole* depend upon a *Part* . . .

He advised the erring critics:

> In ev'ry Work regard the *Writer's End,*
> Since none can compass more than they *Intend.*[40]

By the time of the "Dunciad," some thirty-two years later, Pope found no improvement in the situation:

> The critic Eye, that microscope of Wit,
> Sees hairs and pores, examines bit by bit:
> How parts relate to parts, or they to whole,
> The body's harmony, the beaming soul,
> Are things which Kuster, Burman, Wasse shall see,
> When Man's whole frame is obvious to a *Flea.*[41]

In book 4 of the "Dunciad" Pope again portrayed critics as limiting their concerns to the narrowest confines of philology and hardly capable of moving beyond the level of individual words:

> 'Tis true, on Words is still our whole debate,
> Disputes of *Me* or *Te,* of *aut* or *at,*
> To sound or sink in *cano,* O or A,
> Or give up Cicero to C or K.[42]

Pope's satiric portrayals of the crisis of criticism and the word-bound pursuits of philology supported a line of thought that Watts opposed. Watts addressed the crisis by attempting to defend and refurbish a unified view of philology's multiple chores. For several other writers, however, the dismal state of criticism associated with philology required, in a foreshadowing of romanticism, an act of redemption in which the term "criticism" would be wrested away from philology and assigned to a "higher" activity. One writer who developed this pre-romantic line of thought was Pope's sometime-adversary John Dennis. Dennis's form of departure from the Lockean model of epistemology, in conjunction with his keen interest in Longinus, led him to promote a form of critical reading that would function above and apart from the mundane concerns of philology.

The response Dennis made to the Lockean view of epistemology was quite different from that of Watts, yet it came to be a popular one in the eighteenth century. Writers who made such a response chose not to quarrel with available analyses of the understanding in and of itself. Instead they argued that there were other "neglected parts" of the mind that required attention. In this connection the most popular line of thought associated the neglected parts with the passions and alleged that the passions were far more important than the understanding. Here the quarrel with Locke was not over the characteristics of the understanding but over the relative importance of the understanding and of the passions and their media.

David Hume, of course, was the leading advocate of the primacy of feelings in experience of the world, but before Hume, writers such as Joseph Addison and Francis Hutcheson and the less-well-known John Dennis stirred interest in the "neglected" passions. Hutcheson was a precursor of Hume in analyzing the passions and their role in experience, and he was probably the most influential of those trying to develop a philosophical case for the primacy of feelings. Hutcheson posited an innate moral sense and an innate sense of beauty. Both, he said, were associated initially and predominantly with feelings. His discussions of these two senses and his handling of the theory of association of ideas were probably the most important theoretical treatments of the passions prior to Hume's exposition.

Hume was influenced by Hutcheson's discussion of a moral sense, and in *A Treatise of Human Nature* (1739) and later philosophical-psychological works he upset conventional notions of the interrelations of the passions and reason. As is well known, Hume called the initial dimensions of experience "impressions," which he defined as "sensations, passions and emotions, as they make their first appearance in the soul."[43] He distinguished "impressions" from "ideas." "Ideas" were "faint images of [impressions] in thinking and reasoning."[44] Hume's crucial notion, insofar as theory of reading is concerned, was that "our impressions are the causes of our ideas, not our ideas of our impressions."[45] That John Dennis was an even earlier advocate of a comparable position is commonly overlooked in historical accounts of eighteenth-century developments in rhetoric, logic, and reading.

Dennis's work predated publication of Hutcheson's studies. Dennis was motivated more by educational concerns than by philosophical interests. He believed a fundamental weakness in educational practice was that it concentrated on training the understanding and disregarded training the passions. The education supplement he proposed would emphasize what was commonly referred to as polite learning." In Dennis's view, polite learning addressed the importance of feeling in life and directed educational attention toward developing and improving "taste." Furthermore, a crucial feature of educating the feelings and inculcating taste should be training in a "higher" form of critical reading. It is clear that aesthetic interests more than psychological interests motivated Dennis.

Dennis distinguished between education "which is useful and barely solid, without Ornament" and polite learning. Underscoring the importance of addressing the passions, Dennis found that "of Polite Learning, Poetry appears to be the most . . . attractive Branch, because it is the most moving."[46] He continued, "Poetry . . . excites Passion (and for that very Cause entertains Sense) in order to satisfy and improve, to delight and reform the Mind, and so to make Mankind happier and better: from which it appears that Poetry has two Ends, a subordinate, and a final one."[47] He said, "The subordinate End of Poetry, which is to please, is attain'd by exciting Passion, because everyone who is pleas'd is mov'd, and either desires, or rejoices, or admires, or hopes, or the like."[48] He believed that "poetry attains its final End, which is the reforming of the Minds of Men, by exciting of Passions." Dennis added, "And here I dare be bold to affirm, that all Instruction whatever depends upon Passion."[49]

Ultimately intent upon the reforming powers of poetry, Dennis observed that a properly receptive reader will experience those powers, as well-constructed poetry moves the passions. In his boldest assertion of contrasts between the understanding and the passions Dennis set "the heart" against "the head" and claimed that "a Poet . . . is oblig'd always to speak to the Heart."[50]

Dennis's development of polite learning with its fundamental distinction between the head and the heart reflected two prominent trends. One emerged out of struggles in biblical interpretation; the other was associated with the awakening interest in Longinus to which Dennis contributed. It is obvious that with this background Dennis would differ markedly from Watts in answering the master question about which established intellectual enterprises need to be searched for principles and tools for study of reading. In dealing with biblical interpretation and rhetoric, Dennis thought of those enterprises and their offerings in a manner quite distinct from how Watts conceived them.

Within biblical interpretation there were several versions of what Watts considered a growing tendency, which he opposed, to separate the activity of criticism from the basic activities of grammar and philology. At issue were questions about the extent to which grammatical and philological analysis of human language provided adequate guides to understanding biblical messages and about the extent to which an interpreter must rely on the spiritual guidance of established doctrine or the "inner light" of faith. Extreme versions of spiritually guided interpretation were associated with enthusiastic pietism.

Proponents of religious enthusiasm found the "letter" of a biblical text, as opposed to the "spirit," lifeless. Further, they distrusted the tools for analyzing the letter of the text. They set a vision of spiritual communication between God as ultimate author and the faithful against what they thought of as the narrow intellectual efforts of the grammarians and the philologists. According to this outlook the human language of a biblical text is never fully adequate to its task; language persistently points beyond itself to the idea above the expression. Those who adhered to this view were bound to stress the role of the emotions or passions in spiritual communication.

Secular versions of enthusiastic pietism entered eighteenth-century discussions of reading with the work of Dennis, and these versions had implications similar to those of Ramistic and Lockean forms of reductionism. The assumptions and concerns of enthusiastic pietism and logical-scientific reductionism differed widely, but there was a shared impulse to see what Watts called the common methods of speech as inadequate for the most important forms of communication. Whether that importance was defined in terms of spiritual truth or scientific verifiability, language as customarily used was thought unequal to the tasks of serious communication. Thus at the beginning of the eighteenth century, as now, thinkers raised the issue of whether ordinary language and the means of its analysis were adequate for interpretation and evaluation of serious thought and its communication.

Elements of a secular version of enthusiastic pietism appeared in Dennis's distinction between two sorts of passion, one of which he associated with religious contemplation. Dennis divided passion into "vulgar" and "enthusiastick." Of the former he said, "vulgar Passion, or what we commonly call Passion, is that which is moved by the Objects themselves, or by the Ideas in the ordinary Course of Life; I mean, that common Society which we find in the World."[51] Of the latter he observed, "Enthusiastick Passion, or Enthusiasm, is a Passion which is moved by the Ideas in Contemplation, or the Meditation of things that belong not to common Life. Most of our Thoughts in Meditation are naturally attended by some degree of Passion; and this Passion, if it is strong, I call Enthusiasm."[52] Dennis added that "the strongest Enthusiastick Passions, that are justly and reasonably rais'd, must be rais'd by religious Ideas." A persistent theme in his work is the kinship of poetry and religion as generators of enthusiastic passion, which enabled the best of both poetry and religion to transcend the merely rational, the vulgar, and the mundane.

Dennis's treatment of enthusiastic passion was supported by his interest in what he took to be Longinus's handling of "sublimity" and "transport," concepts Dennis saw as reinforcing his dichotomous treatments of the head and the heart, reason and passion. In moments of enthusiastic passion reason submits to passion and those "who partake of the Transport, are too much shaken to find out Faults."[53] In those moments rational, analytic processing of language would be of little assistance even if it could be exercised, because that which is conveyed is not fully attributed to the language that conveys it. Dennis contended that a segment of discourse that initiates transport "leaves in the Reader an Idea above its Expression."[54]

Like Pope, and others of the period, Dennis was dissatisfied with exclusively philological conceptions of reading, and he was especially concerned with understanding words joined. However, Dennis set for himself the difficult task of providing the reading public with a practical pedagogy for teaching readers how to penetrate and respond to the *sublime*. It was this aspect of Longinus's rhetorical theory and criticism that Dennis valued most highly and that he sought to inculcate in his readers. Indeed, Dennis found *Peri Hupsous* too theoretical, and he chided Longinus for failing to show how a reader's full response to sublimity could be brought about. Since Dennis prized sublime prose and poetry above pragmatic, rational composition and the modes of reading that rationalism invites, he divided critical reading into two kinds, a lower and a higher. The practical, analytical reading that Watts espoused was the lower sort of criticism. Such reading could not penetrate the beauty and nobility of the "best" prose and poetry. To respond fully to such works, said Dennis, a reader must approach texts with openness to what he called "the Spirit of that just Admiration, with which such worthy Thoughts . . . must naturally fill the soul."

Two problems deserve notice here. First, Dennis, without directly admitting the fact, presupposed that readers can somehow know as they come to a text whether or not the higher sort of critical reading is required. His argument was that analytical criticism of the sort Watts praised is legitimate but cannot get at the sublime. That is why rational, analytical reading is insufficient for reading truly important works. But beyond indicating that some subjects, like those with which religion is concerned, are more conducive to the sublime than others, Dennis did not explain how a reader knows which kind of reading a work demands. Second, since Dennis assumed that the sublime exists but is not penetrable by rational philological, and grammatical analysis, he was destined as a pedagogue to face the difficult problem of showing how the "Spirit of just Admiration" could be taught. Both of these problems remained essentially unsolved in Dennis's pedagogy as he struggled to make clear the distinctions between the superiority of the heart over the head and of enthusiastic passion over vulgar passion in reading.

In "The Impartial Critic," Dennis presented a dialogue between Beaumont and Freeman discussing "To the King and his Navy" by Edmund Waller. In this dialogue Dennis subjected parts of Waller's work to a brief but close textual analysis. The method of analysis he presented illustrates what Dennis took to be one task (albeit a mundane one) of a critical reader. Namely, to identify faults in Waller's poem "without being hypercritical." Dennis implicitly warned that in pursuing this form of close textual analysis of poetry, a reader risks ignoring poetry's capacities to "go to the Heart."

In the dialogue's brief exploration of the dividing line between critical and hypercritical reading, Freeman early falls into the "rallery" of hypercriticism:

> *Ships heretofore on Seas, like Fishs sped,*
> *The mightier still upon the smaller fed.*

*Freem.* That is to say, as a great Fish Breakfasts or Dines upon a small one, so a great Ship chops up a little one. I have known several, who, to their sorrows, have seen a Ship drink hard, but I never met with any who have seen one eat yet.

*Beaum.* P'shaw, Pox, this is down-right Banter. This is to fall into the very same fault you have condemned in others.

*Freem.* I stand corrected, Sir; without rallery then, this Metaphor *Feed,* is too gross for a Ship, tho' I perfectly know what Mr. *Waller* means by it.

Freeman makes a more successful pass at the lines:

> *Should Nature's Self invade the World again,*
> *And o're the Center spread the Liquid Main,*
> *Thy Power were safe, and her destructive hand,*
> *Would but enlarge the Bounds of thy Command.*

*Freem.* This is truly sublime indeed; but I have an exception to make to the second Verse. For what does Mr. *Waller* mean, by spreading the Liquid Main o're the Center? The Center is either taken for an imaginary

Point, which is Mathematically in the midst of the Globe, and so to spread any thing over the center cannot be good Sence; or the Center is taken for the whole Globe, consisting of Land and Sea, and then to spread the Main over the Center, is to spread the Center over itself.

*Beaum.* This Criticism seems to be just enough.

*Freem.* Nor am I satisfied with the Epithet Liquid; for every Epithet is to be look'd upon as a Botch, which does not add to the thought. Now it is impossible to think of the Sea, without thinking that it is Liquid at the same time.[55]

The exchanges on the Waller poem provide one sort of model for critical readers, in which the critic approaches literary works using the tools of the head as opposed to those of the heart. This kind of critical reading directs a reader's attention to what Watts referred to as the common methods of speech, an analysis employing the traditional tools of grammar and philology. It is evident from what follows in "The Impartial Critic," and from Dennis's other writings, that Dennis found this sort of critical reading inferior even if legitimate. As he wrote in the prefatory letter of "The Impartial Critic": "For it is much more easie to find Faults, than it is to discern Beauties. To do the first requires but common Sence, but to do the last a Man must have Genius."[56]

When Dennis turned to the more difficult kind of critical reading, his mode of instructing critical readers changed significantly. Readers following the model Dennis presented in "The Grounds of Criticism of Poetry" would, in fact, be held at considerable distance from close scrutiny of the language of the text.

To introduce readers to the "Thoughts, or Ideas, which produce that Enthusiasm which we call Admiration," Dennis indicated that he would turn to examples "that we may show the Reader more plainly how that Spirit [enthusiastic Admiration] is produc'd."[57] However, what Dennis meant by showing "more plainly" had little to do with close textual analysis. In the ensuing presentation Dennis offered relatively long exemplary passages with only minimal commentary. Noting that the reader "will easily see that it derives its Greatness and its Sublimity from the becoming Thoughts which it has of the Deity," Dennis provided the following passage from "Paradise Lost":

> Oh by what Name, for Thou above all these,
> Above Mankind, or ought than Mankind higher
> Surpassest far my naming, how may I

Adore Thee? Author of this Universe,
And all this Good to Man, for whose Well-being
So amply, and with Hands so liberal,
Thou hast provided all things. But with me
I see not who partakes; in Solitude
What Happiness? Who can enjoy alone?
Or all enjoying, what Contentment find?
Thus I presumptuous; and the Vision bright,
As with a Smile more brightned, thus reply'd.[58]

Dennis's comment was: "Here by the way I desire the Reader to observe, how the Spirit of the Poem sinks, when *Adam* comes from God to himself; and how it rises again, when he returns to his Creator. But let us proceed to God's reply."[59] After presenting another long passage, Dennis added the comment: "The reader may easily see, that here is all that is great and sublime in Reason, express'd with the Spirit of that just Admiration, with which such worthy Thoughts of the Deity must naturally fill the Soul."

Dennis's notions of a higher form of critical reading and of a pedagogy of the sublime yielded paradoxes and contradictions. He asserted that readers could easily see the sublimity that was "naturally" produced by treatments of certain subjects, and that to a proper critical reader, one with genius or refined taste, moments of sublimity are self-evident. Why then a pedagogy? It appears that any need for analytic procedures in such cases would be evidence that the reader lacked the genius, the very capacity, for higher critical reading.

Paradoxically, there were occasional instances in which Dennis resorted to close scrutiny of language in his discussions of the higher form of critical reading. For example: "The reader may take notice, that the Comparison of the Sun to *Michael* the Prince of the Arch-Angels, is admirably liken'd to the top of the invisible creation." Such analytical observations are rare in his work, but they are present. For the most part, however, he held that the higher form of critical reading requires genius to appreciate transport in the sublime. A reader so equipped seems to suspend close scrutiny of language and direct his or her energies toward enthusiastic admiration of the lofty thoughts by which "the Soul [is led] to its Maker."[60] The circularity of Dennis's thought produced a closed conception of reading in which reading is equated with appreciation, but for which there is no pedagogy for identifying the means of appreciation except through exposure to discourse that deserves appreciation!

An ideal of appreciation unfettered by analysis appeared again in Dennis's discussion of what Longinus treated as the third mark of the sublime. "It leaves in the Reader an Idea above its Expression," Dennis said of that third mark. "Now no Expressions can come up to the Ideas which we draw from the Attributes of God, or from his wondrous Works, which only the Author of them can comprehend."[61] The general uselessness of lower critical reading and its tools of analysis are made manifest by such statements.

Dennis's observations, like those of Watts, indicated that rhetoric was an established intellectual enterprise to which the study of reading could turn. However, the two writers differed radically in their perception of what was to be selected from rhetoric. Watts appealed to rhetoric for information about structural features of discourse, which he found in a range of figures construed as the common methods of speech. Dennis went to rhetoric for information about what he considered to be a select class of figures associated not with the common methods of speech, but with the passions and sublimity. Dennis believed that the heart and the passions have distinctive "natural" linguistic media. In "The Grounds of Criticism" he wrote that "the figurative Language is but a Consequence of the Enthusiasm, that being the natural language of the Passions."[62]

By subjecting figurative language to the dichotomy of head and heart Dennis established two classes of figurative language. One class included "Point and Conceit, and all they call Wit." This kind of figuration Dennis declared "to be for ever banish'd from true Poetry: because he who uses it, speaks to the Head alone." The other class, which was "simple and natural," could "go to the Heart; and Nature (humanly speaking) can be touch'd by itself alone."[63]

That division, again in keeping with Dennis's response to the Lockean epistemological model, located the first kind of figures in the province of the lower, common-sense form of critical reading. That he banished these figures from "true poetry" and the higher form of critical reading indicates his reasons for not discussing that class of figures. The rarefied, "simple and natural" figures must include species of metaphor, we can infer from Dennis's examples. However, Dennis was little inclined to discuss the particulars of the higher class of figures. That disinclination was consistent with his perception that the higher form of criticism and the objects of its view were not amenable to mundane analysis. Thus the student of higher critical reading was left believing that certain figures were crucial to production of the sublime but with questions about what those figures were at best only partially answered. How those figures operated remained one of the mysteries of nature.

In the battle of the books, Dennis clearly sided with the new ancients. The interests of grammar, and many of those of rhetoric, were separated from serious critical reading. What remained maintained its position only so long as it did not involve what Dennis saw as mundane, common-sense analysis.

The contrasts between Watts and Dennis as theorists of reading were sharp. Watts's unified view of reading as an activity licensed a pragmatic conception of figures as strategic instrumentalities basic to all verbal communication. It was a conception warranted by his modification of Lockean epistemology. As he turned to rhetoric for assistance, Watts developed a pragmatic view that led him to explore both the traditional rhetorical category of style and the relationships between style and arrangement, or *dispositio*. His key-word theory and pedagogy of reading left much unelaborated, but driven by his pragmatic conception of discourse, that theory and pedagogy began the work of providing students with analytical procedures for reading. Especially helpful were his directions that readers should search for the meanings of key words *in relation to one another* and be guided in that search by an awareness of how the structures of figures such as antithesis could influence overall meaning.

In contrast, Dennis offered a bifurcated view of reading that denigrated pragmatic conceptions of discourse and isolated critical reading as a form of appreciation available only to genius. This segmentation was warranted by his reaction to Lockean epistemology. Dennis thought Locke had adequately handled the faculty of understanding and its methods of communication. Dennis supplemented Locke by taking as his own special province those faculties associated with emotions, which he believed were the faculties that enabled people to perceive and respond to sublimity.

The kind of critical reading Dennis espoused foreshadowed later discussions of "taste" and later romantic defenses of aestheticism. When Dennis looked to rhetoric for help, his aestheticism led him to focus on rhetorical postulates quite different from those that interested Watts. What Dennis found significant in rhetorical theory was a conception that only certain figures could produce sublimity and only certain subjects allowed tasteful use of those figures. Since he prized the mystery of transport, of capturing the idea above the expression, he offered minimal discussion of *how* such figures operate in language and on the mind.

Bonamee Dobree and David Morris, among others, have identified Dennis as a figure who influenced the later shape of English criticism. Morris credits Dennis with being "the first English critic to make sublimity the keystone of his poetics."[64] It also seems clear that Dennis's treatment of sublimity in relation to his theory of a higher form of critical reading encouraged later romantic views of criticism in general.

One comment Morris makes about Dennis underscores the major difference between Watts and Dennis. Referring to the kind of "literary analysis" Dennis applied to biblical poetry, Morris says, "Dennis did not speak of rhetorical terms." He displayed model passages to illustrate sublimity and, presumably, to inculcate receptivity to the sublime, but he stopped there. It was Watts who undertook to explain *how* figuration could appeal in special ways and be used strategically.

The extensive differences between the basic views of Watts and Dennis rendered their general conception of education divergent. Watts's emphasis on the roles of the common methods of speech and his insistence on the unity of comprehension and criticism in reading were in harmony with his and others' attempts to inculcate literacy in the populace. Dennis's emphasis on higher critical reading implied that if reading were truly worthwhile, it was beyond the grasp of the public and could not be shared with them. For him and any who followed his line of thinking, the common methods of speech and the means of analyzing them were scarcely worth an educator's attention.

Dennis's premises and postulates could only lead him to an elitist conception of reading. Watts's premises and postulates led to a democratization of literacy and to practical, public education in reading. The divergence of the two men's theories and practices point up fundamental tensions that affected theories of reading well into the nineteenth century.

NOTES TO CHAPTER 2

1. Anne S. Pratt, *Isaac Watts' Gifts of Books to Yale College* (New Haven, Conn.: Yale University Press, 1938), p. 68.
2. *The Works of Isaac Watts*, D. Jennings and P. Doddridge, eds. (London: J. Barfield, 1810), vol. 5, p. 539.
3. Watts, *Works*, vol. 5, p. 540.
4. Watts, *Works*, vol. 5, p. 21.
5. Watts, *Works*, vol. 5, p. 21.
6. Watts, *Works*, vol. 5, p. 540.
7. Watts, *Works*, vol. 5, p. 537.
8. Watts, *Works*, vol. 5, p. 537.
9. Watts, *Works*, vol. 5, p. 23.
10. Watts, *Works*, vol. 5, p. 29.
11. Watts, *Works*, vol. 5, p. 30.
12. Watts, *Works*, vol. 5, p. 39.

13. Watts, *Works,* vol. 5, p. 39.
14. Watts, *Works,* vol. 5, p. 173.
15. Watts, *Works,* vol. 4, p. 700.
16. Watts, *Works,* vol. 4, p. 700.
17. Watts, *Works,* vol. 5, p. 661.
18. Murray Cohen, *Sensible Words: Linguistic Practice in England, 1640–1785* (Baltimore, Md.: The Johns Hopkins University Press, 1974), p. 10.
19. Watts, *Works,* vol. 4, p. 698.
20. Watts, *Works,* vol. 4, p. 700.
21. Cohen, *Words,* p. 119.
22. Wilbur Samuel Howell, *Eighteenth–Century British Logic and Rhetoric* (Princeton, N.J.: Princeton University Press, 1971), p. 112.
23. Wilbur Samuel Howell, *Logic and Rhetoric in England, 1500–1700* (New York: Russell and Russell, 1956), p. 328.
24. Lawrence Manley, *Convention* (Cambridge: Harvard University Press, 1980), p. 188.
25. Paul de Man, "The Epistemology of Metaphor," in *On Metaphor,* ed. Sheldon Sacks (Chicago: University of Chicago Press, 1978), pp. 20ff.
26. Watts, *Works,* vol. 4, p. 415.
27. Watts, *Works,* vol. 5. p. 166.
28. Watts, *Works,* vol. 5. p. 259.
29. Watts, *Works,* vol. 5. p. 169.
30. Watts, *Works,* vol. 5. p. 169.
31. Watts, *Works,* vol. 5. p. 170.
32. Watts, *Works,* vol. 5. p. 174.
33. Watts, *Works,* vol. 5. p. 230.
34. Watts, *Works,* vol. 5. p. 228.
35. Watts, *Works,* vol. 5. p. 316.
36. Watts, *Works,* vol. 1. p. xxiii.
37. Watts, *Works,* vol. 4, p. 682.
38. Watts, *Works,* vol. 4, p. 680.
39. Watts, *Works,* vol. 4, p. 681.
40. Alexander Pope, *Poetry and Prose of Alexander Pope,* ed. Aubrey Williams (New York: Houghton Mifflin Company, 1969), pp. 44–45.
41. Pope, *Poetry,* p. 364.
42. Pope, *Poetry,* p. 363.
43. David Hume, *A Treatise of Human Nature,* ed. L. A. Selby-Bigge (1739; Oxford: Oxford University Press, 1978), p. 1.
44. Hume, *Treatise,* p. 1.
45. Hume, *Treatise,* p. 5.
46. John Dennis, *The Critical Works,* ed. Edward Niles Hooker (Baltimore, Md.: The Johns Hopkins University Press, 1939), vol. 1, p. 205.
47. Dennis, *Works,* vol. 1, p. 336.
48. Dennis, *Works,* vol. 1, p. 337.
49. Dennis, *Works,* vol. 1, p. 337.
50. Dennis, *Works,* vol. 1, p. 127.
51. Dennis, *Works,* vol. 1, p. 338.
52. Dennis, *Works,* vol. 1, p. 338.
53. Dennis, *Works,* vol. 1, p. 135.

54. Dennis, *Works,* vol. 1, p. 360.
55. Dennis, *Works,* vol. 1, pp. 24–27.
56. Dennis, *Works,* vol. 1, p. 13.
57. Dennis, *Works,* vol. 1, p. 341.
58. Dennis, *Works,* vol. 1, pp. 342–43.
59. Dennis, *Works,* vol. 1, p. 343.
60. Dennis, *Works,* vol. 1, p. 348.
61. Dennis, *Works,* vol. 1, p. 360.
62. Dennis, *Works,* vol. 1, p. 359.
63. Dennis, *Works,* vol. 1, p. 127.
64. David B. Morris, *The Religious Sublime* (Lexington: University of Kentucky Press, 1972), p. 55.

# 3

# TWO VIEWS OF
# READERS' RESPONSE

John Mason, author of *An Essay on Elocution and Pronunciation,*
wrote the second English manual in the art-of-reading tradition. He gave
little attention to the theoretical implications of the positions he took,
but his slender, widely circulated manual touched on many theoretical
and pedagogical issues with which later studies of reading contended
more directly.

Mason knew of Watts's work and cited the *Art of Reading and Writing
English*. He shared Watts's interest in tapping the resources of traditional
rhetoric in order to create a contemporary model for training in reading.
He also agreed with Watts that training for basic comprehension and
training for critical reading were not separable enterprises. Furthermore,
Mason envisioned a course of training in reading that would give the
populace an opportunity to attain the highest forms of literacy, as did
Watts.

In respect to the Lockean epistemological model, however, Mason
stood with Dennis. Mason was among several writers in the eighteenth
century who contended that Locke may have accounted well for the nature of understanding but had left unattended very important and "neglected parts of the mind."

To the master question, To which established intellectual enterprises
should one turn to borrow models or principles for an independent study
of reading? Mason would have answered, "above all, rhetoric." However,
what Mason saw as valuable in rhetoric was not quite what Watts saw,
nor was it what Dennis saw. Mason was intent upon those aspects of
rhetoric that were associated with the term "oratory." He was primarily
concerned with "elocution" as "a Branch of Oratory, the Power and Im-

portance of which is greater than is generally thought; insomuch that Eloquence takes it's [sic] Name from it."[1] Given the highly oral implications of theory of oratory, it was to be expected that the master question about relationships between the spoken and the written forms of language prominently concerned Mason.

Mason's particular interest in oral reading was linked to his response to the Lockean epistemological model. Translating his view of an epistemological problem into an observation about what he considered a widespread pedagogical problem, Mason asserted that current educational attempts to develop and improve the understanding were supported at the expense of other vital "powers and operations" of the "human mind." He believed that few students had been trained to "have the right government of their passions," and he warned that "he who does not improve his Temper, together with his Understanding, is not the much better for [his education]."[2] These observations appeared in *A Treatise on Self-Knowledge,* which was published approximately three years before the printing of the *Essay on Elocution.*

Mason saw the study of oral reading as an ideal discipline for training the whole mind and as a discipline concerned with education of the passions as well as the understanding. Mason saw spoken language as the avenue to the neglected parts of mind because speech was the primary medium of expression of feelings and attitudes: "Thus the different Passions of the Mind are to be expressed by a different Sound or Tone of Voice. *Love,* by a soft, smooth, languishing Voice; *Anger,* by a strong, vehement, and elevated Voice."[3] Mason believed that studying the characteristics of spoken language would reveal the complexities of the various types and degrees of the passions. This understanding would, in turn, allow deeper and fuller comprehension of the written word.

This suggests that education of the understanding also was to be attained by concentrating on oral expression. The understanding would be exercised in trying to discover and reexpress the meaning of what was read. Mason referred to this meaning as authorial "sense." He wrote: "If you would acquire a just Pronunciation in Reading you must not only take in the full Sense, but enter into the Spirit of your Author."[4] This was the ideal value that Mason envisioned for the study of oral reading.

However, the ideal as he presented it masked problems that later writers uncovered. One problem was, what actual relationship exists between the written and the spoken forms of language? Mason clearly, if implicitly, treated the spoken language as by far the richer and more complete form of language. Speech could convey the operations of the understanding, and it could also convey the passions through "sound or Tone of

Voice." Mason also assumed that written language could, at least in principle, be translated into spoken form without losing any of the meanings that writing can convey. However, whereas Watts assumed a basically symmetrical relationship between written and spoken forms and so had no difficulties in supposing comprehensive "translations," Mason saw difficulties in "translating" what he conceived as essentially unsymmetrical forms of expression. Although Mason did not draw attention to the matter, his tinkerings with what he considered the nuances of translation reveal some of the very serious problems that later thinkers confronted when they tried to work out the interrelationships of written and spoken discourse.

One such problem arose when Mason said that a reader must discern the author's intentions, which he insisted must be of primary concern to an oral reader. "A good Pronunciation *in reading,*" Mason wrote, is

> the Art of managing and governing the Voice so as to express the full Sense and Spirit of your Author in that just, decent, and graceful Manner, which will not only instruct but affect the Hearers; and will not only raise in them the same Ideas he intended to convey, but the same Passions he really felt.[5]

For all this, Mason recognized that obstacles must be overcome before the reader's grasp of authorial sense and spirit could be translated into oral form.

Mason's treatment of punctuation illustrates the problems he faced in trying to teach how authors' intentions were to be divined. The "common stops or Points" (comma, semicolon, colon, period, admiration) were presented as major guides to meanings and intentions. Their function is to "distinguish the Sense of the Author." At first Mason portrayed the common stops as fairly reliable guides. He noted, cautiously, "You will in a good measure in reading be directed by the Points: but not perfectly; for there are but few Books that are exactly pointed."[6] A little later in his discussion, Mason admitted that the reliability of the points as guides was rather questionable: "But after all, there is so much License admitted, and so much Irregularity introduced, into the modern Method of Punctuation, that it is become a very imperfect Rule."[7]

Mason was reflecting his skepticism about the written word as a medium of expression. He thereby introduced into eighteenth-century thought about reading the problem of whether there is actually a fundamental division between idea and expression in communication. When Dennis touched on this issue, he said that in the highest form of critical reading an idea could be greater than the expression used to convey it, though this mode of reading presupposed that readers had taste and genius. In Dennis's view, written and oral communications were equally amenable to the "easier" and more pedestrian critical analysis using tools of philology and grammar. By contrast, Mason's work reveals a line of thought implying that spoken and written languages have fundamentally different communicative potentialities, regardless of the kind of reading or hearing given them. It is therefore Mason who first called into question previous assumptions in the eighteenth-century study of reading about the stability and communicative powers of printed texts.

As Mason worried about the unstable and enfeebled forms of expression on which authors have to rely when communicating in print, he also reflected the instability of his concept of sense. Like Watts, Mason held that a reader's major goal was to discover authorial sense, that is, the author's intended meaning. However, as he aired his frustrations concerning the "modern Method of Punctuation," Mason gave the term "sense" a meaning quite different from "authorial sense." He said a reader's search for the meanings that punctuation conveys "must be chiefly regulated by a careful Attention to the Sense and Importance of the Subject."[8] Here sense was not exclusively an author's expressed sense of his or her meaning. When grammatical pointing supplied insufficient guidance to the author's intended sense, a reader was to fall back on his or her own sense of the subject and its importance. In a problematic situation, Mason would let the reader turn from the author's stylistic cues and search the subject itself for clues to the probable meaning of the text. Although Mason apparently did not realize it, his advice opened the way for arguments that readers are, at least sometimes, better judges of meanings than authors—a possibility much discussed and still unsettled today.

The ambiguity of the term "sense" in Mason's manual illustrates the tensive cohabitation of "older" and "newer" conceptions of style. Mason subscribed to the newer view when he directed his students to search for the writer's "attitudes toward or understanding of his subject." However, given the unreliability of punctuation, readers might have to fall back to a conception of style as the "pattern of language appropriate to the subject of the discourse."

The importance of the tension between the older and newer conceptions of style was further manifest in Mason's treatment of emphasis. Mason's characterization of emphasis was similar to that provided by Watts. Mason noticed that "the Voice must express, as near as may be,

the very Sense or Idea designed to be conveyed by the emphatical Word."
He added:

> the emphatical Words (for there is often more than one) in a Sen-
> tence are those which carry a Weight or Importance in themselves,
> or those on which the Sense of the rest depends; and these must
> always be distinguished by a fuller and stronger Sound of Voice,
> wherever they are found, whether in the Beginning, Middle, or
> End of a Sentence.[9]

To illustrate how emphatic words are discovered, Mason provided the
following couplet from Pope and added accent marks as indicators of the
seats of emphasis:

> Get Plăce and Wĕalth, if possible with Grăce,
> If not by ăny Means get Wĕalth and Plăce.

The example relies heavily on structures of opposition, which Watts had
found to be important guides in determining emphasis. However, Mason
did not comment on the functions of oppositional structures in a reader's
discovery of the seats of emphasis. He simply said, "In these Lines the
emphatical Words are accented; and which they are the Sense will always
discover."

Mason's example with marks was to stand as an illustration of emphatic patterns representative of authorial sense, intention, or design.
However, as students moved beyond Mason's manual to other forms of
sentences in printed discourse, they faced several difficulties. One was
the erratic use of pointing that Mason noted. Faced with that difficulty,
readers were to revert to another conception of style and to the second
notion of sense—they must use their own senses of the subject and its
importance. This position introduced a highly controversial role for the
reader. According to some later writers, readers who followed only their
own senses of the subject exercised dangerous license in the vital activity
of placing emphasis. Such license might permit readers to arrive not at
authorial meaning but at reader's meaning. Guided only by his or her
sense of the subject, a reader might usurp the role of the author and
become a rewriter of the text.

Mason had a response to this fear, but it was one with which opponents of his position were not comfortable. It was also one that brought
to the fore in eighteenth-century reading studies issues growing out of the

differences between the older rhetorical conception of emphasis and the newer linguistic view of emphasis. Watts had allied himself with the older rhetorical notion of emphasis, which did not presuppose significant differences between the written and spoken forms of language. He had done this by noting that the dispositional features of rhetorical figures such as antithetical structures should be counted among the common methods of speech by which authors display patterns of emphasis in written form.

Mason, in contrast, was driven by his distrust of the communicative powers of the written language. He embraced the newer linguistic sense of emphasis and made it basic to his theory and pedagogy of reading. Mason directed his students to attend to "common conversation." There they would find that certain subjects trigger passions that in turn guide an oral reader to certain associated tones. In other words, conventions of oral expression of thoughts and feelings should guide readers. Mason wrote, "If we are indeed deeply affected with the Subject we read or talk of, the Voice will naturally vary according to the Passion excited."[10] The distinction between Mason's and Watts's views is clear: to discover clues to what deserves emphasis, Watts would have his reader study the author's rhetorical *dispositio,* but Mason would have his reader study the passional expressiveness of conventional users of the language.

What Mason found in a knowledge of conversational language was a system of safeguards for the reader. Readers well versed in the spoken language as it is ordinarily used would know how certain subjects were typically communicated, whether specific clues to authorial design were available or not. Thus Mason asserted, "In reading then attend to your Subject, and deliver it just in such a Manner as you would do if you were talking of it." The notion that a reserve fund of knowledge, with its stock subjects and passions, can guide accurate expression was derived from the older belief that style is the pattern of language appropriate to the subject of the discourse and as Cohen notes, was a notion consistent with a definition of language that stresses correlation between language and things.

Mason believed that his manual borrowed from and advanced several of the central principles in Watts's textbook. There were surface similarities in the books, but they masked very important differences. A fundamental difference was that Mason worked from an "utterance notion" of contextual meaning, whereas Watts worked from a key-word notion of meaning. The importance of this difference can be illustrated by considering the following advice from the two authors, Mason advised: "In reading then attend to your Subject, and deliver it just in such a Manner as you would do if you were talking of it."[11] Watts said: "Let the tone and sound of your voice in *reading* be the same as it is in *speaking.*" The two bits of advice appear similar, but in fact they are not. Watts was offering counsel on how to translate into the oral mode meaning that a reader had discovered *in writing* by means of following certain clues that a *writer* had provided in a *text*. Mason was writing under the presupposition that speech is rich in clues to meaning and writing is enfeebled. Mason was telling readers to discover *textual* meaning by experimenting with *oral* clues. How the writing could be *uttered* was the guide to its meaning. In this sense it can be said that with the publication of Mason's manual, there were in the art-of-reading tradition two divergent theories of the process: Watts's conception of reading for contextual meaning by using clues provided by authors' usages in their texts and Mason's conception of reading "with the ear" because of the limited clues to meanings that writing is capable of conveying.

In explaining reading, Mason formally declared the primacy of oral language. He thereby raised a question that has troubled theories of reading ever since: What are the interrelationships of written language and spoken language? The position Mason took is still with us, as can be seen from Ong's twentieth-century claim:

> Written texts all have to be related to sound somehow, directly or indirectly to the world of sound, the natural habitat of language, to yield their meanings. "Reading" a text means converting it to sound aloud or in the imagination.[12]

Mason's or Ong's conception of the fundamental natures of written and oral languages is at odds with conceptions of writing implicit in the views of Watts and other theorists. Mason was perhaps unique in dealing with rhetoric as a discipline from which reading theory should borrow. Mason conceived rhetoric as the theory of the art of *oratory*. Many theorists who were willing to draw on rhetorical principles, including Isaac Watts, denied that this was a proper understanding of rhetoric as a source of useful principles.

Mason's manual was brief in part because oratory and "common conversation" rather than written texts held the clues to effective reading. The vital lessons learned from observing oral discourse would not be derived from textbook rules for analyzing *texts*. For Mason, as for Dennis, there was little to be gained from philological-grammatical analysis. But in the absence of a source of systematic analysis, Mason was led to posit that some people have a natural ability for reading and some do not. In so saying, Mason was not far from Dennis's position that serious reading is a matter of genius. Some students, Mason observed,

> can more readily enter into the Sense and Sentiments of an Author, and more easily deliver their own, than others can; and at the same Time have a more happy Facility of expressing all the proper Variations and Modulations of the Voice than others have. Thus Persons of a quick Apprehension, and a brisk flow of animal Spirits (setting aside all Impediments of the Organs) have generally a more lively, just, and natural Elocution than Persons of a slow Perception and a flegmatic Cast.[13]

Mason thus allied himself with the position that in reading, nature is more powerful than nurture. Although he had begun with the same goal as Watts, that of training the populace to the highest degree of literacy, his presupposition that natural ability was crucial seriously weakened the prospects of attaining that goal. In the end, excellence in literary understanding was more a gift than something earned by study.

NOTES TO CHAPTER 3

1. John Mason, *An Essay on Elocution and Pronunciation* (1748; reprint Menston, England: The Scolar Press, 1968), p 3.
2. John Mason, *Self-Knowledge: A Treatise* (London: James Buckland, 1778), p. xi.
3. Mason, *Essay*, p. 26.
4. Mason, *Essay*, p. 28.
5. Mason, *Essay*, pp. 19–20.
6. Mason, *Essay*, p. 21.
7. Mason, *Essay*, p. 23.
8. Mason, *Essay*, p. 23.
9. Mason, *Essay*, pp. 23–24.
10. Mason, *Essay*, p. 18.
11. Mason, *Essay*, p. 18.
12. Walter J. Ong. *Orality and Literacy* (London: Methuen, 1982), p. 8.
13. Mason, *Essay*, p. 20.

# WRITER'S MEANING OR
# READER'S MEANING

Near the middle of the eighteenth century there was a flurry of activity in the study of reading. Several of the issues raised by Isaac Watts, John Dennis, and John Mason were newly and sometimes dramatically examined by writers concerned with the art of reading. Between mid-century and the early 1760s there were appeals to and modifications of the two rival conceptions of reading: the one that grew out of Watts's key-word view of contextual meaning, and the one that was built on Mason's utterance notion of contextual meaning. Theorists and pedagogues also responded to Dennis's program for teaching critical reading.

Mid-century theorists and pedagogues inherited the problem of whether critical reading and reading for comprehension were separate or interrelated enterprises. Dennis had propagated the notions that instruction in critical reading was distinct from instruction in reading for comprehension and that the chief end of the former should be to improve readers' tastes and judgments. As mid-century writers were aware, Dennis's view had been opposed by persons who treated reading as a unified activity that improved taste and judgment as comprehension was pedagogically improved. For this purpose, reading at ascending levels of written material had been the chief pedagogy proposed.

Those who adhered to the notion that reading was a unified activity were prone to applaud the classical model of rhetorical training wherein virtues and vices of style were given direct attention and the development of taste and judgment was a natural outcome. This response, however, still left at issue the proper way to construe rhetoric. On this point there had been a fundamental difference between Watts's view of rhetoric as a supplement to the study of reading and the "oratorical" view of rhetoric held by Mason.

Two mid-century writers who are sometimes described as "elocution-ists" attempted to flesh out a theory of reading using an utterance notion of meaning rather like that which Mason had adopted. Thomas Sheridan and James Burgh offered extensions and reworkings of this concep-tion of reading and contextual meaning. Neither found any need to separate study of critical reading from study of reading for comprehen-sion because, as Sheridan said, the eventual results of a properly con-ceived basic reading program would be "to diffuse a general good taste thro' the nation."[1]

Both Sheridan and Burgh shared with Dennis and Mason the view that Lockean epistemology "neglected parts of the mind," primarily the passions and their media of communication. Their modification of Locke's analysis was distantly related to Hume's way of handling the relationships between the passions and the understanding. Hume in-cluded the passions in that class of "impressions" of which "ideas" are the "faint images . . . in thinking and reasoning." Thus Hume assigned the passions a fundamental and vital role in the activities of the mind, and so did Burgh and Sheridan. However, Sheridan and Burgh made a more striking claim than did Hume, namely, that the passions were linked with "intention." As Burgh indicated and Sheridan later echoed, it is the "Passions and Humors" to which "intention or sentiments of the mind" must be traced.

Associating passion and intention holds out some hope of discovering a link between the understanding and the neglected parts of the mind. In the hands of Sheridan and Burgh, however, rivalry between the under-standing and the passions and their separate media was intensified. Since Sheridan's views were far more elaborately articulated and had wider impact than Burgh's, I have taken as my primary point of reference Sheri-dan's version of a theory and pedagogy of reading based on an utterance notion of contextual meaning.

Sheridan's quarrel with Locke was similar to, but more explicit and strident than, Dennis's and Mason's calls for more attention to capacities beyond the understanding. Sheridan argued, as had others, that Locke's failure lay in confining his examination to only one "part" of the mind, and he chided Locke for not extending his analysis to other neglected parts. In Sheridan's view a major problem created by Locke's failure had been development of a tacit assumption that Locke's treatment of the understanding accounted for the *most important* part of the mind and the most important operations of language. Sheridan contended that what was needed was an analysis and description of those parts of mind that were more important than the understanding. He did not, however, complain of Locke's accomplishments.

Crediting Locke with having "treated his subject with the utmost precision, and perspicuity," Sheridan observed:

> Is it not amazing to reflect, that from the creation of the world, there was no part of the human mind clearly delineated, till within the last sixty years? when Mr. Locke arose, to give us a just view, of one part of our internal frame, "the understanding," upon principles of philosophy founded on reason and experience.[2]

Sheridan praised Locke for his "discovery" that "it is impossible we can think with precision, till we first examine whether we have precise ideas annexed to . . . terms: and it is equally impossible to communicate our thoughts to others with exactness, unless we are first agreed in the exact meaning of our words."[3]

Sheridan acknowledged that Locke had warned that the "abuse of words" will cease only when due consideration is given to the "regulation" of the meanings of words that function as the "marks of ideas." At this point, Sheridan's praise came to a rather abrupt halt, and he asked: "But do men think, or reason more clearly, than they did before the publication of that book [Locke's *Essay*]? Have we a more precise use of language, or are the number of verbal disputes lessened?" Sheridan charged that "little or no benefit in point of practice, has resulted from a display in theory, of the only part of the human mind, which has hitherto been laid open with accuracy, upon principles of true philosophy."[4] Sheridan's charge of impracticality is a reminder that a persistent theme in most discussions of the art of reading was the necessity of turning theoretical explorations to practical pedagogical benefit.

Sheridan found that, as a model for an exploration of parts of the mind beyond understanding and for an exploration of the media of those parts, the *Essay Concerning Human Understanding* was both inadequate and misleading. He contended that beyond the understanding

> there are two other parts of the human mind, with regard to which the world is at this day, as much in the dark, as they were with respect to the whole, previous to the publication of Mr. Locke's essay: The one, the seat of the passions; for which we have no name existing in the mind, unphilosophically referring it to the organ of sensation, the heart: the other, the seat of the fancy; which is called the imagination.[5]

Sheridan added that "upon a right regulation of these parts of the mind, and the faculties belonging to them, all that is noble and praiseworthy, all that is elegant and delightful, in man, considered as a social being, chiefly depends."

Sheridan announced his intention to base the study of reading on a proper appreciation of differences between the spoken and the written forms of language. In one formulation, Sheridan's distinction harkened back to discussions by Mason and to positions held by some grammarians earlier in the century. Sheridan proposed to show "the spoken language, as it ought to be, the archetype; of which, the written language should be considered only as the type."[6] As Sheridan proceeded, however, the relationship of archetype to type gave way to a far more starkly dichotomous view of speaking and writing.

In developing his discussion of the powers of the spoken form of language and of oral reading, Sheridan made a distinction unprecedented in the eighteenth-century study of reading. He asserted the separateness of "two different kinds of language" that are in "utter independence of each other" and that have "no sort of affinity between them, but what arises from an habitual association of ideas."[7] This distinction and the ensuing discussion of the two separate kinds of language offered a dramatic alternative to one assumption that underlay Watts's art of reading, namely, that the spoken and the written forms of language were fundamentally compatible.

Sheridan showed little restraint in his praise of the power of spoken language. He deemed the spoken language "the immediate gift of God, who has annexed to it (when cultivated by man) powers almost miraculous, and an energy nearly divine. He had given to it tones to charm the ear, and penetrate the heart; he has joined to it action, and looks, to move the inmost soul . . . . Persuasion is ever it's [sic] attendant, and the passions own it for a master."[8] Sheridan, like Dennis, gave attention to the relation of speech to religious passion, though this quotation indicates that religion was simply one of many enterprises dependent on the speech-passion interconnection. Sheridan referred to "the wild uncultivated oratory of our Methodist preachers" and commented that "it may be doubted whether all the passions together have greater power over the mind of man than enthusiasm alone."[9] Sheridan's general point was that the "gift of God" was the form of language most suited to stirring feelings of all sorts.

Burgh's defense of the spoken language directly associated this mode of communicating with sublimity of the "highest" sort. He said that the spoken language is capable of sublimity "which does not wait for cool *approbation.* Like irresistible *beauty,* it *transports,* it *ravishes,* it *commands* the *admiration* of *all,* who are within its reach. If it allows *time* to *criticise,* it is not *genuine.*"[10] Here was an application of Longinian terms that went considerably beyond Dennis's conceptions.

The association of the passions and the spoken form of language intensified the contrast between the vast communicative powers of oral reading and the enfeebled activity of silent reading. Sheridan was, indeed, the first English writer on the art of reading to articulate a clear distinction between "silent reading" and "reading aloud," and the weaknesses he found in the written language were directly associated with the hazards he found in silent reading. The distinction between the two kinds of reading appeared in Sheridan's *Course of Lectures on Elocution* (1762). There he proposed to "lay open the sources of our errors and faults in the art of reading; partly arising from the unskillfulness of masters, and partly from defects and imperfections in the very art of writing itself."[11]

Among the defects of the written language that Sheridan discussed was one that had troubled Mason: writing's inability to provide all of the "visible marks" necessary for an oral reader's "just delivery of a text." Sheridan defined a "just delivery" as "a distinct articulation of words, pronounced in proper tones, suitably varied to the sense, and the emotions of the mind; with due observation of accent; of emphasis, in its several gradations; of rests or pauses of the voice, in proper places and well measured degrees of time; and the whole accompanied with expressive looks, and significant gesture." Sheridan believed the written language could provide only two rudimentary clues to delivery. It could indicate "articulate sounds or words, which are marked by letters; and stops or pauses of the voice, which are marked by little figures and tittles [*sic*].[12]

Like his predecessors discussing the art of reading, Sheridan saw the matter of determining emphasis as a crucial problem in reading. According to him, one of the major weaknesses of written language was that neither accent nor emphasis could be clearly communicated by writing. By accent he meant, as he said in the book's third lecture, "a peculiar manner of distinguishing one syllable of a word from the rest."[13] Accent is also "the chief mark by which words are distinguished from mere syllables."[14] He qualified the last remark with, "Or rather I may say, it is the very essence of words, which without that, would be only so many collections of syllables."

In the fourth lecture Sheridan explained his conceptions of emphasis. He began the lecture by observing that "emphasis, discharges in sentences, the same kind of office, that accent does in words." His claims for accent and emphasis at this point are worth noting in some detail:

> As accent, is the link which ties syllables together, and forms them into words; so emphasis, unites words together, and forms them into sentences, or members of sentences. As accent, dignifies the syllable on which it is laid, and makes it more distinguished by the ear than the rest; so emphasis, ennobles the word to which it belongs, and presents it in a stronger light to the understanding. Accent, is the mark which distinguishes words from each other, as simple types of our ideas, without reference to their agreement or disagreement: Emphasis, is the mark which points out their several degrees of relationship, and the rank which they hold in the mind. Accent, addresses itself to the ear only; emphasis, thro' the ear, to the understanding. Were there no accents, words would be resolved into their original syllables: Were there no emphasis, sentences would be resolved into their original words.[15]

While Sheridan's accounts of accent and emphasis were more boldly stated than those of earlier writers on the art of reading, what gained the attention of his later detractors was not his view of accent and emphasis in isolation, but what he found to be the relationship between that view and his concept of the two "utterly independent kinds of language."

Near the end of the fourth lecture, Sheridan examined the problem of accent and emphasis in relation to silently reading the written language. A reader is presented with "no visible signs but letters and stops, and as the words are distinguished from each other, only by a greater distance between them than between the letters which compose them; and the different members of sentences, by little crooked figures; the eye has no assistance in the two most important parts of reading, accent and emphasis."[16] Soon after these comments, Sheridan intensified his assault on written language, arguing that it was

> a mistake, which men naturally enough fall into, who judge of language only in its written state; that sentences are wholly composed of words and stops, because there are no other visible marks offered to the eye; but the man who considers language in its primary and noblest state, as offered to the ear, will find that the very life and soul of speech, consists in what is utterly unnoticed in writing, in accent and emphasis.[17]

On this point Sheridan's detractors cried "foul." Sheridan's utterance notion of contextual meaning asserted with some vehemence that the execution of spoken language is required in order to join words fully together into discourse. To assert that emphasis "unites words together and forms them into sentences" and to find emphasis "utterly unnoticed in writing" was, as Sheridan's opponents recognized, to cut deeply into the belief that a written or printed text is even minimally trustworthy as a conveyor of authorial meaning.

The ways in which Sheridan and Burgh applied their utterance notion of contextual meaning had drastic implications for what I have called the rhetorical sense of emphasis. If emphasis cannot be conveyed in writing, then structures such as rhetorical figures cannot exist as clues to authorial meaning. Sheridan's and Burgh's declarations implied that emphasis is *force applied by a speaker or reader.* The reader, not the author, determines emphasis and, hence, meaning.

Sheridan's attack on the written language was especially vigorous. He contended that the kind of language that served the understanding was the "dead letter," the language of "words." This language was very different from what he called "the language of the passions and the fancy," which was "utterly independent of words" and was constituted by tones and gestures.[18] He insisted that Locke's influential examination of the language of the understanding had contributed to "an early false bias given to us in our system of education, and afterwards continued thro' life; I mean that extravagant idea entertained of the power of writing, far beyond what in its nature it can ever attain."[19]

It was natural enough that Sheridan's minimization of what writing could attain fueled fires of controversy among students of reading. Watts had begun an art-of-reading tradition with the assumption that printed discourse is capable of conveying authorial intentions and meaning. A reader was to search texts for clues to authorial design. Sheridan and Burgh flatly denied Watts's basic assumption. However, as we shall see, Watts was not without theoretical successors.

Sheridan, in keeping with his various distinctions between the written and the spoken language, the dead letter and the living voice, employed a distinction between "meaning" and "full meaning." In his usage meaning, as associated with the understanding, is available through the written language and is concerned, as Locke had pointed out, with the relationship between the word and the idea for which it stands. Full meaning, however, is associated with the whole mind and, with its reliance on "tones," fully available only to the spoken language, and it is vitally concerned with words joined. In Sheridan's words:

All that passes in the mind of man may be reduced to two classes, which I shall call, Ideas and Emotions. By ideas, I mean, all thoughts which rise and pass, in succession in the mind of man: by emotions, all exertions of the mind in arranging, combining, and separating its ideas; as well as all the effects produced on the mind itself, by those ideas, from the more violent agitation of the passions, to the calmer feelings, produced by the operation of the intellect and fancy. In short, thought is the object of the one: internal feeling of the other. That which serves to express the former, I call the language of ideas; and the latter, the language of emotions. Words are the signs of the one; tones, of the other.[20]

For Burgh as well as Sheridan, the index of meaning, design, or intention was fully available only in the medium of spoken language. Burgh believed that intention was associated with the passions, whose medium was the spoken language. That position was underscored in Sheridan's characterization of emotions as "the exertions of the mind in arranging, combining and separating its ideas" and in Sheridan's insistence that the spoken language was the medium of the emotions. The full implications of this view were expressed by Burgh, who said, "What we mean does not so much depend upon the words we speak, as on our *manner* of speaking them" (my emphasis). Under this view writing was denied full communication even to the understanding.

Burgh's approach to reading escaped the most radical implications of Sheridan's articulation of the utterance notion of contextual meaning, but only because Burgh offered nothing more than a version of John Mason's position, that of depending on the older conception of style. Burgh's skepticism about the communicative powers of print and about criteria for judging authorial "manner" strongly informs his attempt to direct students to consider the "matter" of discourse. Burgh noted that in his textbook on oral reading he had "put together a competent *variety* of *passages* out of some of the best writers in prose and verse, for exercising youth in adapting their general manner of delivery to the *spirit* or *humour* of the various matter."[21] Burgh's instructions to students referred not to authorial design, but to matter. For example, in discussing the flaws of a chanting sort of reading, Burgh informed students that chant is "unnatural, because the continually varying strain of the *matter* necessarily requires a continually varying series of *sounds* to express it." He added that "cant, or monotony, in expressing the various matter of a discourse, do not in the least *humour* the matters they are applied to; but on the contrary, confound it."[22]

84

Burgh required his student, as Mason had required his, to concentrate on subject matter that would, in ways not made very clear, engender the corresponding emotion. Burgh devoted a large portion of his manual to the problem of properly conveying emotion or passion. He did not equivocate: "Nature has given to every emotion of the mind its *proper* outward expression, in such a manner, that what suits *one*, cannot by any means, be accommodated to *another*."[23] This kind of one-to-one relation of emotion to manner of presentation became a staple claim for such nineteenth-century elocutionists as the followers of François Delsarte; the important point is that Burgh did not deal with how a reader discovers *which* emotions are conveyed by the words joined in a particular text.

As help to readers seeking meanings in discourse, Burgh's analysis was seriously wanting. To validate his claim that each emotion has its peculiar manner of vocal expression, Burgh provided a list of more than seventy of "the principal *passions, humours, sentiments,* and *intentions,* which are to be expressed by *speech* and *action,*" and he gave a summary of the "manner" in which "*nature* expresses them."[24] Discovery of emotional meanings in words joined was apparently to come about by a reader's consulting his or her own common sense—sense well honed by those processes so often recommended by romantic literary criticism and theory, namely, "study models and study nature."

Sheridan did not directly invoke the formula of studying the matter, but he did agree with Burgh that there were "universal" or "uniform" ways of expressing particular subject matters. Burgh and others were committed to the older notion of style that presupposed that certain subjects "naturally" produced certain emotions. Sheridan did not make this claim. Instead, he said, the language of the passions has been "impressed, by the unerring hand of nature on the human frame." Sheridan would have his readers believe that whatever the emotional response, the form of its expression is universally recognized. Even if this were true, Sheridan, like Burgh, was omitting consideration of how to discriminate one emotional response from another. And given the chasm Sheridan found between the potentialities of oral and written languages, it is difficult indeed to find answers to the question, How does a reader determine from the *printed* language of the text *which* universally intelligible emotion is to be conveyed by the words joined? The older notion of style led Mason and Burgh to the position that the reader was to consult his or her own sense—a highly problematic one, but an answer of sorts. Sheridan did not take even this position. Having expatiated on the limited meanings perceivable in written language, he left his readers with no methods at all for interpreting written material, which was the impoverished relic of living, informing, oral language. If what Sheridan had said about written language were true, there would be no passion at all conveyed through that medium. What, then, was a reader to do when confronted, say, with a lyric in print?

Writers on reading who insisted that their pupils become students of customary use, including Watts and Mason, accepted a principle that foreshadowed modern versions of Ferdinand de Saussure's *langue-parole* distinction and Noam Chomsky's competence-performance distinction. Common to Saussure's concept of *langue* and Chomsky's notion of competence is the view that the experienced speaker of a language has acquired an elaborate fund of information about the rules governing that language. While for most speakers this information remains largely unarticulated, it serves as a powerful guide in their uses of the language.

Versions of *langue* and of competence have emerged in recent theories of reading as apparent guards against an ultimate relativism in which each reader's response to a given text is unique and unrelated to other readers' responses to the same text. Stanley Fish, for example, grants that in no two readers are "the responding mechanisms exactly alike," but he rejects the argument that "because of the uniqueness of the individual, generalization about [readers'] response is impossible." That rejection is founded on Fish's acceptance of the principle of linguistic competence: " 'The idea that it is possible to characterize a linguistic system that every speaker shares.' "[25]

Early eighteenth-century precursors of the notion of competence and twentieth-century versions of *langue* and competence share the assumption that there is a minimally viable, representative relationship between the spoken and the written forms of language. That is not to say that twentieth-century adherents to the notion of competence would find the relationship between speaking and writing as nonproblematic as Watts found it. From classical to modern times, persons who have thought seriously about the relationships between speaking and writing have found writing a relatively feeble representation of speech. Plato condemned writing in the *Phaedrus* and Saussure treated writing as an often guileful "technical device or external accessory that need not be taken into consideration when studying language."[26] Indeed, it is in part due to Saussure that the idea of writing as a weak representation of speech has been dominant in twentieth-century linguistics. However, even for Plato and Saussure, writing does reflect speech, no matter how weakly. It can *mean* both literally and figuratively.

86

Sheridan posed a crucial question to his contemporaries who held an early version of the competence notion. The question arose from the extent to which he dispossessed writing of intentional meanings. As his later detractors rightly perceived, his theory of emphasis denied that writing could give access to some of the most important "messages" associated with oral meaning, those pertaining to the intentions of the user of the language. Thus a staple of what we now call a view of competence was suddenly exploded by Sheridan's analysis, with serious consequences to writers on reading in the eighteenth century and later.

Sheridan's views forced writers on reading to give new thought to the relationships between the spoken and the written forms of language. Jacques Derrida recently called into question the long-popular model in which speech is the basic system of which writing is an imperfect representation. As I show in the next chapter, some early writers on reading found themselves making similar challenges to Sheridan's theses. For the present, it is sufficient to observe that the doctrines of Sheridan and Burgh forced thinkers who valued the written word for itself to reconsider the difficult questions of how printed texts convey meaning and of what printed texts can say and what they must leave unsaid. Given the prominence of Sheridan's writings, it was to be expected that these problems received high priority in the study of reading during the second half of the eighteenth century. Sheridan's doubters began to argue that the printed form of language has a healthy life of its own, independent of the spoken form.

By the end of the 1760s the issue of educability had also become a crucial one for writers on reading. The belief that educability in reading is more the province of nature than of pedagogy originated with Mason and was reinforced by Burgh and Sheridan. In the minds of Burgh and Sheridan, educability in reading depended centrally upon a reader's natural ability to observe and absorb the rich, multiple, but relatively standard patterns of the spoken form of English. Opponents of this view needed to recover and refurbish the view that Watts had held in primitive form: that the common methods of speech include structurations (as in antithesis and other figures) that provide clues to authorial designs.

NOTES TO CHAPTER 4

1. Thomas Sheridan, *A Course of Lectures on Elocution* (1762; reprint, Menston, England: The Scolar Press, 1971), pp. xi–xii.
2. Sheridan, *Course,* pp. vi, v.
3. Sheridan, *Course,* p. vi.

4. Sheridan, *Course*, p. ix.

5. Sheridan, *Course*, p. ix.

6. Sheridan, *Course*, p. 235.

7. Sheridan, *Course*, p. 7.

8. Thomas Sheridan, *British Education: Or, the Source of the Disorders of Great Britain* (1756; reprint, New York: Garland, 1970), pp. 63–64.

9. Sheridan, *Education*, p. 116.

10. James Burgh, *The Art of Speaking*, p. 208. The portions of the text of Burgh's *Art of Reading* referred to in this chapter are those that appear as the final section (under the title *On Public Speaking*) of Sheridan's *Rhetorical Grammar of the English Tongue* (1781; reprint, Menston, England: The Scolar press, 1969), in which Burgh is not cited as the author.

11. Sheridan, *Course*, p. 6.

12. Sheridan, *Course*, p. 10.

13. Sheridan, *Course*, p. 41.

14. Sheridan, *Course*, p. 44.

15. Sheridan, *Course*, p. 57.

16. Sheridan, *Course*, p. 70.

17. Sheridan, *Course*, p. 71.

18. Sheridan, *Course*, p. x.

19. Sheridan, *Course*, p. xii.

20. Sheridan, *Rhetorical Grammar*, p. 100.

21. Burgh, *Speaking*, p. 160.

22. Burgh, *Speaking*, pp. 169–70.

23. Burgh, *Speaking*, p. 177.

24. Burgh, *Speaking*, pp. 180ff.

25. Stanley Fish, "Literature in the Reader: Affective Stylistics," in *Reader-Response Criticism*, ed. Jane Tompkins, (Baltimore, Md.: The Johns Hopkins University Press, 1980), p. 83.

26. Jonathan Culler, *On Deconstruction: Theory and Criticism after Structuralism*, (Ithaca, N.Y.: Cornell University Press, 1982), p. 100.

# 5

# PRAGMATISM VERSUS
# BELLETRISM

Robert Lowth, Joseph Priestley, George Campbell, Lord Kames (Henry Home), and Hugh Blair were important contributors to a debate that is often described as a struggle between classicism and romanticism. The work of Kames is dealt with prominently in histories of criticism, and the work of Blair tends to be viewed as an important series of documents in the history of rhetoric. Both, however, reflected and refined early romantic impulses that had appeared in the work of John Dennis. Kames and Blair, like Dennis, found in Longinus an ancient kindred spirit. Their readings of Longinus inspired them to explore the means by which "taste" and "genius" break the constraints of classical rules. Kames and Blair were not the first English proponents of romantic versions of thought about critical reading, but their popular and widely read works invigorated an eighteenth-century predilection for a romantic version of critical reading.

A divergent direction for the study of critical reading appeared in the work of Lowth, Priestley, and Campbell. While the work of Kames and Blair fit well within the traditional categories of romanticism and classicism, the work of Lowth, Priestley, and Campbell set out its problems in terms not reducible to classical and romantic characterizations. Lowth, for instance, was highly influenced by Longinus, but he advocated a view of critical reading quite different from that of Kames and Blair. What Lowth, Priestley, and Campbell offered was a new version of the pragmatic theory of critical reading that first appeared in the discussions of Watts.

Several historians have observed that Lowth and Priestley were major contributors to English grammar's mid-century shift to a new and extensive exploration of syntax. Further, these historians assert that Lowth,

Priestley, and Campbell were instrumental in directing interest away from the postulate that an ideal or natural syntactic model exists, and toward concern with the varying patterns of customary use. In relation to the latter point, Murray Cohen has indicated the essential agreement of Lowth, Priestley, and Campbell. Cohen notes Lowth's recognition of the fact that "to discuss the grammar of any known language requires the application of the principles of grammar 'to that particular language, according to the established usage and custom of it.' "[1] He also cites Priestley's warning that "linguists themselves must 'conform to established vicious practices, if [they] would not make [them]selves justly ridiculous by [their] singularity.' "[2] Further, Cohen refers to Campbell's occasional reliance on Priestley. One such point of reliance is the following observation by Campbell in *The Philosophy of Rhetoric*: "I entirely agree with Doctor Priestley, that it will never be the arbitrary rules of any man, or body of men whatever, that will ascertain the language, there being no other dictator here but use."[3]

Discussing English grammar's mid-century shift in emphasis, Cohen describes a premise shared by those heavily concerned with syntax, namely, "the relation between language and the mind." Cohen continues:

> However, the linguists do not discuss the operations of language in terms of the operations of the mind: that is, they drop the logical analysis of syntax. Instead, they revive the seventeenth-century technique of associating linguistic features with a parallel scheme. Their scheme, however, is not the order of things predicated by seventeenth-century linguists, but another aspect of language— manners of speaking. They discuss the relation between mind and language rather than language and nature and do that in stylistic rather than in logical terms.[4]

If we substitute "rhetorical" for "stylistic" in Cohen's last sentence, Cohen's comments are even more enlightening. Cohen himself makes that substitution when he says, "Priestley uses the assumption that thinking is a linguistic activity to get to the rhetorical variations that mark different expressions of thought."[5] In short, for Priestley, Lowth, and Campbell rhetorical objectives justify manipulations of English syntax. Cohen observes that "once syntactic features become the distinctive aspects of speech in this new way, then mental habits can easily be characterized by stylistic traits."[6] This "new way" was the employment of rhetorical figures and tropes to formulate patterns of "words joined" and the closely related patterns of thought. Lowth, Priestley, and Campbell all assumed that a close relationship existed between thought and language, and for all three the structures of certain rhetorical figures seemed to illustrate that relationship.

In their attitudes toward the processes of reading critically, Lowth, Priestley, and Campbell followed the tradition of thought first expressed by Isaac Watts. As had Watts, these mid-century writers held that common methods of speech, including rhetorical figures, were used *strategically* by writers and therefore that critical interpretation of texts was an integral part of comprehending texts. Their conclusions have special significance because of the stature of these three men in the literary-philosophical world and because of the lasting influence of their thinking—which does not mean, of course, that their conceptions were universally accepted. For example, their contemporary Kames construed Longinus much as Dennis had, and so he arrived at the view that reading to comprehend and reading critically were separate operations of the mind.

What is remarkable about the similarities among the conclusions of Lowth, Priestley, and Campbell is the diversity of the epistemological assumptions from which they proceeded. Lowth moved from the view that the Lockean model needed to be supplemented, a view also held by Dennis, John Mason, James Burgh, and Thomas Sheridan. Priestley's observations proceeded from a form of materialism more sympathetic to the Lockean model than to the modification of it by Watts. Campbell, who with Thomas Reid was prominent in the so-called Scottish Common Sense Movement, worked from a common-sense epistemological view that attempted to correct the Lockean model in a manner much like that adopted by Watts.

Divergent as these starting points were, all three men agreed on the fundamental assumption that multiple patterns of language are closely related to multiple patterns of thought. All three, like Watts before them, supported the newer conception of style. This assumption led Lowth, Priestley, and Campbell to explore in detail patterns of syntax and the patterns of figuration, and to see these various patterns as essential manifestations of thought. Thus Lowth, Priestley, and Campbell offered "rhetoric" as one prominent answer to the question of where the study of reading should turn for supplementary principles and tools. The three also shared a strong interest in biblical interpretation and translation. All wrote and lectured on biblical interpretation, and all were concerned with the relationships between principles of secular critical reading and principles of biblical interpretation.

Several observations fundamental to Lowth's view of critical reading are contained in his lectures titled *Praelectiones de Sacra Poesi Hebraeorum* and in his later preface to the translations of *Isaiah*. Scholars have persistently and rightly suggested that Lowth's lectures hold a rather special place in some larger context. For example, Norman Maclean asserts that Lowth returned the British Longinian tradition of literary concerns to considerations of the medium, especially of matters pertaining to language and style.[7] Similarly, Samuel Monk has suggested that Lowth set for himself a more limited aim than did his Longinian predecessors and contemporaries, an aim that "held him fast to criticism" and "precluded the possibility of developing a thorough aesthetic system."[8] In discussing the published lectures in the context of biblical interpretation, Hans Frei notes that Lowth's work "was so carefully confined to formal analysis that despite the warm reception it was accorded it made little difference to any other type of interpretation."[9] However, these lectures have long seemed special not only because Lowth was concerned with the relationship between secular and biblical criticism, but also because elements of his theory and pedagogy stand in a rather anomalous relationship to Longinian literary theory and to biblical interpretation in his own time, even while Lowth clearly perpetuated interests of the English Longinian tradition.

Lowth shared with Dennis a practical pedagogical interest in training for critical reading, but Lowth did not make Dennis's distinction between an easier and a more difficult mode of critical reading. He did not posit a form of reading that depends on common sense and a form that depends on genius. Rather, his lectures were intended to exemplify what Lowth identified as an attempt to embrace all "the Great Principles of General Criticism" and to offer a "compendium of all the best rules of taste." Where Dennis had found disparity between two kinds of critical reading and among the capacities of readers, Lowth saw continuity. In this sense his lectures constituted a return to the position of Watts, in which the activity of criticism cannot be separated from various "philological" activities, including close grammatical and rhetorical analysis.

Lowth's attention to the "medium" returned the English Longinian tradition, after a period of some neglect, to a concern with close scrutiny of language. More important, his pedagogy rested on a conception of the medium that was sympathetic to notions of language that were then in some disfavor among other adherents to the Longinian tradition. Whereas Dennis thought of the higher form of critical reading as ultimately intent on discovering the idea above its expression, Lowth persistently guided his students of the sublime toward close scrutiny of the forms of expression that produce poetic effects, including the sublime. In his lectures Lowth called attention to "three modes of ornament" of "most frequent use, namely, the amplification of the same ideas, the accumulation of others, and the opposition or antithesis of such as are contrary to each other." The role that such conceptions of style-as-*dispositio* had in certain earlier writings on theory of critical reading was considerably increased in Lowth's hands.

Dennis had largely consigned scrutiny of rhetorical forms and strategies to the "easier" form of criticism. By contrast, Lowth, in his lectures and in the preface to the translation of *Isaiah,* was intent on guiding critical readers and translators toward identifiable forms of expression. In his preface Lowth wrote that "strict attention to form and fashion of the composition" is useful to a translator and is also of "great use to him likewise merely as an Interpreter; and will often lead him into the meaning of obscure words and phrases." This conception considerably broadened notions about what could be learned from the forms and structures of written discourse. In the same preface Lowth provided a forceful example of how a reader can penetrate written discourse through close attention to what Lowth characterized as the "parallel" forms of expression:

The next verse gives us an instance still more remarkable of the influence which the Parallelism has in determining the sense of the words:

We have entered into a covenant with death;
And with the grave we have made— ה צ ח

what? Everyone must answer immediately an agreement, a bargain, a treaty, or something to the same sense: and so in effect say all the versions, ancient and modern. But the word means no such thing in any part of the Bible; (except in the 18th verse of this Chapter, here quoted, where it is repeated in the same sense, and nearly in the same form;) nor can the Lexicographers give any satisfactory account of the word in this sense; which however they are forced to admit from the necessity of the case; . . . It could not otherwise have been known, that the word had this meaning; it is the Parallelism alone, that determines it to this meaning; and that so clearly, that no doubt at all remains concerning the sense of the passage.[10]

93

Lowth left no doubt about where the path of close scrutiny of typical "forms of expression" led:

> For whatever senses are supposed to be included in the Prophet's words, Spiritual, Mystical, Allegorical, Analogical, or the like, they must all entirely depend on the Literal Sense. This is the only foundation upon which such interpretation can be securely raised; and if this is not firmly and well established, all that is built upon it will fall to the ground.[11]

The warning to critical readers was double-edged, applying to both a religious and a secular reading. It constituted a caution against the excesses of enthusiastic pietism's approaches to biblical interpretation and against a secular form of critical reading that champions the idea above its expression.

Where Dennis had taken idea-above-the-expression to be a staple of Longinian transport, Lowth's conception of critical reading implied that all forms of reading proceed from recognition of the vital interdependence of thought and expression. This represented adherence to the newer view of style. In fact, Lowth said of style, "the meaning of this word I do not wish to be restricted to the diction only of the sacred poets, but rather to include their sentiment, their mode of thinking."[12]

Lowth presented a forceful counterreform for the theory of critical reading. The counterreform moved in opposition to reading schemes, like those of Dennis, Mason, Sheridan, and Burgh, that proceeded from distrust of the common methods of speech or distrust of the written or printed form of language and of the traditional tools and methods of interpreting the common methods of speech used in writing.

Priestley's version of the counterreform was also based on a belief in the close association of thought and language. This is shown in his sweeping observation:

> The correspondence between every person's thoughts and language is perhaps more strict, and universal, than is generally imagined: For since there can be but few perceptions or ideas existing in the human mind, which were not, in their very rise, and first impression, associated with the words that denote them; it is almost impossible, but that ideas and the symbols, or expressions of them, must arise in the mind at the same time.[13]

94

This observation considerably expanded Watts's defense of the common methods of speech as trustworthy and essential conveyors of the operations of the mind.

Priestley also saw that the structures of language and the structures of rhetorical figures and tropes were scarcely separable. In his grammar he asserted, with a flourish:

> And whither can we, with less deviation from the principles of language, go for their embellishment, than to the source from which the greatest part of all languages was derived. For the forms of expression that are not, ultimately, more or less figurative, are much fewer than is generally apprehended.[14]

Of metaphor he said, "Metaphors do not only constitute the principal part of writings, calculated to please, but even the Metaphysician and Philosopher are obliged to borrow a little of their aid."[15] These observations resemble Watts's comments on structures of figurative language, but Priestley greatly enlarged the conception of figuration and its meanings by insisting that all forms of language partake of figuration in some degree.

In examining the characteristics of figurative language, Priestley articulated a theme that also reverberated clearly in the writings of George Campbell. Priestley took the position that because thought and language are closely associated, and because the structures of figures and tropes are central features of language, one must systematically explore rhetorical figures and tropes. In discussing "contrast," for example, Priestley pointed out that contrast was variously used "and branched out, into a great variety of pleasing scenes, by varying the *subjects* and the *degrees* of it."[16] He added:

> To this we must not only allow the considerable share that hath been ascribed to it in *metaphors* . . . but must acknowledge that we are principally indebted to it for the pleasure we receive from *antithesis,* from objects that are *risible,* or *ridiculous,* from the *mock-heroic, burlesque, parody, irony, repartee, wit, humour, riddles,* and *puns*; with many others entertainments of the same kind, for which we have no distinct name.[17]

As he discussed contrast and the many ways it is used in discourse, Priestley pointed directly at the limitations of criticism as it was currently practiced. Criticism simply was not allowing in its accounts for the many *kinds* of contrasts actually used. He wrote: "the terms of criticism do . . . little correspond to all the varieties of the divisions and subdivisions of this copious subject [contrast], and have been used with . . . little uniformity and precision by critics."[18] The remark attacked the narrowness of current critical practice and implied that closer examination must be made of language in which thought is conveyed.

One reason Priestley thought close analysis was imperative was that readers must search stylistic usages for clues to authorial design. He deplored the "conceit, the spleen, and the petulance, of critics in language and the *Belles Lettres*." To avoid such pitfalls, readers must be trained to judge whether or not *"the manner of writing . . . adequately expresses the whole of what is intended."*[19] Readers must, he said in the *Course of Lectures in Oratory and Criticism,* learn to "distinguish the character of the *design*" of a composition and to "judge how far the execution is adapted to the undertaking."[20] Design was to be discovered and its execution judged by attending closely to the forms used in writing and their communicative adequacy for the purpose.

Priestley's insistence that thoughts can be expressed many different ways led him into conflict with generic criticism as a substitute for close grammatical-rhetorical analysis of texts. He chided critics for bringing prior expectations about genre to particular works being read. "Established criticism" had been "too hasty in establishing general laws of writing from particular instances of successful composition."[21] Good writing, Priestley insisted, was replete with unpredictable usage. At the conclusion of a lively account of how modern writers skillfully evaded the "rules," he said:

> And all the rules of *Epic* writing are dispensed with, and all the uses of such works preserved, in the looser dress of a *Novel* or *Romance*: from each of which, being executed with all imaginable diversity of manner (owing to the human genius being left to its native freedom, in a province as yet uninvaded, at least unoccupied, by the critics) the spirit of ancient commentators, might have established quite different sets of rules for this species of composition.[22]

Expressed in modern terms, Priestley was demanding that critical readers approach each text afresh and evaluate it *on its own terms*. All critical reading must recognize that the infinite diversity of the subjects of human enquiry and speculation, might suggest an infinite diversity in the very kinds of composition, and that the diversity of light in which the same subject may be viewed by different human intellects, might occasion as great differences in the manner of treating them.[23]

In all of the observations Priestley was dealing with critical reading and was challenging the reductionist approaches to reading, as Watts had earlier challenged Ramistic reductionism. Now, however, the "enemy" was belletristic and generic reductionism.

Priestley's linking of judgment and the search for authorial design, as in his directives to "distinguish the character of the design" and "judge how far the execution is adapted to the undertaking," allowed him, more clearly and steadfastly than his predecessors, to articulate the ultimate inseparability of critical reading and reading for comprehension. Both activities must use the tools that permit close scrutiny of the language, including the structures of rhetorical figures, through which the particular thought of a particular author is manifest.

George Campbell's version of the counterreform bore some significant resemblances to Priestley's. Further, Campbell's acceptance of an epistemological model in which "common sense" was an "original source of knowledge common to mankind," and in which the mind's "power of abstracting" was evident "as early as the use of speech," gave his concept of critical reading a foundation very similar to that of Watts.[24]

For Campbell, as for Priestley, the close association of thought and language was a central fact. Campbell believed that "language and thought, like body and soul, are made to correspond, and the qualities of one exactly to cooperate with the other." Through "habitual use" and the "regular structure of a language" the "connexion among signs is conceived as analogous to that which subsisteth among their archetypes" in nature, Campbell wrote, concluding that "we really think by signs as well as speak by them."[25]

In examining the characteristics of language that correspond to thought, Campbell firmly asserted that attention to structures, including those of rhetorical figures and tropes, was essential to speakers, writers, listeners, and readers. At the conclusion of his discussion of tropes in *The Philosophy of Rhetoric*, Campbell observed that tropes "are so far from being the inventions of art, that, on the contrary, they result from the original and essential principles of the human mind."[26] This was perhaps the strongest assertion of a principle that had been emerging in theory of reading since the work of Watts.

Campbell noted that not enough had been done to trace "figures to the springs in human nature from which they flow."[27] He further observed that "the names that have been given are but few, and by consequence very generical. Each class, the metaphor and the metonymy in particular, is capable of being divided into several tribes, to which no names have yet been assigned."[28]

In Campbell's view a thorough knowledge of the structures in "general" or "customary" use in any language was necessary for any form of reading, especially critical reading. This principle linked Campbell's conceptions of critical reading of secular and of sacred texts. In the preface to his translation (with preliminary dissertation) of the four gospels Campbell outlined a program for biblical interpretation grounded in the principles that guide secular critical reading:

> As to . . . the meaning of the revelation given;—if God has condescended to employ any human language in revealing his will to men, he has, by employing such an instrument, given us reason to conclude, that, by the established rules of interpretation in that language, his meaning must be interpreted; otherwise the use of the language could answer no end, but either to confound or deceive. If the words of God were to be interpreted by another set of rules than that which the grammar of the language, founded in general use, presents us; with no propriety could it be said that the divine will is revealed to us, till there were a new revelation furnishing us with a key for unlocking the old.[29]

Campbell's directions for critically reading sacred texts centered on methods for searching out the design or intention of the human writers of those texts. One of his three general directions was "to consider the principal scope of the book, and the particulars chiefly observable in the method by which the writer has proposed to execute his design." Another general rule was to "endeavour to get acquainted with each writer's style, and as he proceeds in the examination, to observe his manner of composition, both in sentences and in paragraphs."[30]

As he stressed attending to the design of the human author, Campbell took issue with a commonly used guideline to interpreting biblical texts, the "analogy of faith." He said:

> If no more were meant by making the analogy of faith the rule of interpreting, than that, where an expression is either dark or equivocal, an interpretation were not to be adopted which would contradict the sentiments of the writer, manifestly declared in other

passages perfectly clear and unequivocal; this is no more than what candour would allow in interpreting any profane author who seems to have enjoyed the exercise of his reason.[31]

However, said Campbell, the analogy of faith was too often employed to square interpretations with sets of beliefs that the reader already held.

Campbell's reservations about the analogy of faith are on much the same footing as Priestley's concerns about readers' prior conceptions of genre. Both were reservations about one or another of the manifestations of searching for ideas above their expressions. It seemed to Campbell that the analogy of faith was too often employed as a tool for imposing prior expectations, and as a substitute for the vital close scrutiny of the language through which authorial design would be conveyed.

Critical reading had a different fate in the hands of Kames and Blair. Both of these men perpetuated Longinian concern with the sublime, and both were intent upon laying out the principles of a "science." For Kames the "rational science" was criticism that promises to improve the taste and judgment of those who attend carefully to the fundamental principles of the "fine arts" and the principles of human nature from which they are drawn. Blair distinguished between rhetoric as a "practical art" and as a "speculative science," both of which were his concerns. He said of the speculative science that "the same instructions which assist others in composing, will assist them in judging of, and relishing, the beauties of composition."[32] As he explored the concept of criticism identified with rhetoric as a speculative science, Blair offered a distinction reminiscent of Dennis's distinction between the higher and the lower forms of critical reading:

> As rhetoric has been sometimes thought to signify nothing more than the scholastic study of words, and phrases, and tropes, so criticism has been considered as merely the art of finding faults; as the frigid application of certain technical terms, by means of which persons are taught to cavil and censure in a learned manner. But this is the criticism of pedants only. True criticism is a liberal and humane art. It is the offspring of a good sense and refined taste. It aims at acquiring a just discernment of the real merit of authors.[33]

Kames made a broader but similar distinction between the pursuits of those with refined taste and those without it. He noted that faults and failings will be obvious to "the man upon whom nature and culture have bestowed this blessing [taste] . . . but these he avoids or removes out of sight, because they give him pain." "On the other hand," he added, "a man, void of taste, upon whom even striking beauties make but a faint impression . . . loves to brood over errors and blemishes."[34]

Both Kames and Blair believed that natural objects with the proper characteristics trigger emotions of sublimity in persons of taste. Refined taste allows beauty and sublimity, in nature and in art, to have their powerful effects on the emotions and the passions. Monk has observed that for Blair "in external objects the simplest form of grandeur is found in the vast and boundless prospects of nature, for all vastness produces the impression of sublimity."[35] One of Monk's comments about Kames is also applicable to Blair: "The mind, it is assumed, responds automatically and consistently to certain classes of objects; introduce these objects into a poem or a painting and you have the sublime."[36] If one qualifies Monk's rather impatient observation by adding that the objects must be properly introduced, his characterization holds for both Kames and Blair.

A version of how a properly constructed poem came to stand as the medium through which objects in nature trigger appropriate responses in a reader is found in Blair's treatment of James Thomson's "The Seasons":

> [Thomson] had studied, and copied nature with care. Enamoured of her beauties, he not only described them properly, but felt their impression with strong sensibility. The impression which he felt, he transmits to his Readers; and no person of taste can peruse any one of his Seasons, without having the ideas and feelings which belong to that season, recalled, and rendered present to his mind.[37]

The poem succeeded by atuning the responses of the reader to the object in nature.

As Blair put the matter, a properly constructed poem would function as a medium for presenting a properly sensitive reader with an object in nature. The question of *how* this happens went unanswered. In this respect Blair held a conception that language functions autonomically. This was not unlike the conceptions of Mason, Burgh, and Sheridan. It is the utterance notion of contextual meaning, elements of which were directly asserted by Kames:

> The natural signs of emotions, voluntary and involuntary, being nearly the same in all men, form an universal language, which no

distance of place, no difference of tribe, no diversity of tongue, can darken or render doubtful.

And Kames added:

> . . . each passion, or class of passions, hath its peculiar signs; and, with respect to the present subject, it must be added, that these invariably make certain impressions on a spectator: the external signs of joy, for example, produce a cheerful emotion.[38]

From this general view of language, Kames derived directions for readers, and they were very similar to Mason's position that the reader should consult his or her own sense. Kames said:

> The only general rule that can be given for directing the pronunciation, is, To sound the words in such a manner as to imitate the things they signify. In pronouncing words signifying what is elevated, the voice ought to be raised above its ordinary tone; and words signifying dejection of mind, ought to be pronounced in a low note. To imitate a stern and impetuous passion, the words ought to be pronounced rough and loud; a sweet and kindly passion, on the contrary, ought to be imitated by a soft and melodious tone of voice: in Dryden's ode of *Alexander's Feast,* the line *Faln, faln, faln, faln,* represents a gradual sinking of the mind; and therefore is pronounced with a falling voice by everyone of taste, without instruction.[39]

Kames's version of the utterance notion of contextual meaning drew upon and tended to perpetuate the older notion that style is "the pattern of language appropriate to the subject of the discourse."

A reader committed to the utterance notion of contextual meaning is unlikely to engage in close philological, grammatical, or rhetorical analysis of linguistic methods. The factors at issue become "appropriateness" and "taste," neither of which is readily open to practical analysis. For Kames the utterance notion led to a conception of critical reading much like that of Dennis. Indeed, several of the antipragmatic, elitist impulses visible in Dennis's idea of critical reading were intensified in Kames's early version of aestheticism and in Blair's conceptions of rhetoric and belles lettres. In Kames's terms, training in true criticism, as opposed to the "criticism of pedants," should be given to "the man upon whom nature and culture have bestowed" at least some degree of "delicate and discerning taste." The steps in educating critical readers therefore involved primarily refining their taste and sensibilities.

For Kames and for Blair, as much as for Dennis, this refinement was to be accomplished largely through repeated exposure to models, that is, passages of discourse that have achieved such qualities as sublimity or beauty. Through such exposure students of critical reading would become sensitive to the impressions passed from objects in nature through properly sensitive writers and properly constructed discourse. The heart of the pedagogy of belletristic critical reading was the display of models with minimal commentary on the pragmatics of how the language of the passages worked.

In the rarefied realm of this "science" of criticism, where readers of the most refined taste encountered examples of beauty and sublimity, the act of critical reading was, as it was for Dennis in higher critical reading, more reaction than action. It was transport, a version of arriving at the idea above the expression. The ultimate "act" of critical reading in the new science of criticism could even be reverie. Kames said, "The reader's passions are never sensibly moved, till he be thrown into a kind of reverie; in which state, forgetting that he is reading, he conceives every incident as passing in his presence, precisely as if he were an eyewitness."[40] Particularly in the work of Kames, the utterance notion of contextual meaning contributed to a radical skepticism about the status of textual meaning. It contributed to the paradox in which the most privileged acts of critical reading are inactions.

When those advocating the new science of criticism turned their attention to figures and tropes, they refined Dennis's earlier distinction between figures of the head and those of the heart. The writings of Kames and Blair sharpened the disagreement between the pragmatic and the aesthetic strains of theory and pedagogy of critical reading, so that the difference was even more extensive than that which had existed between the views of Watts and Dennis.

Kames and Blair advanced beyond Dennis's discussion by more systematically classifying those figures that belonged to the passions, isolating them from those that belonged, in Blair's phrase, to the mere "parade of speech." Kames said about this task:

> The endless variety of expressions brought under the head of tropes and figures by ancient critics and grammarians, makes it evident, that they had no precise criterion for distinguishing tropes and figures from plain language. It was accordingly my opinion, that little could be made of them in the way of rational criticism;

till discovering, by a sort of accident, that many of them depend on principles formerly explained, I gladly embrace the opportunity to show the influence of these principles where it would be the least expected. Confining myself therefore to such figures, I am luckily freed from much trash; without dropping, as far as I remember, any trope or figure that merits a proper name.[41]

He then discussed figures such as metaphor, allegory, personification, apostrophe, and hyperbole.

Blair said of his plan for distinguishing among figures:

If we attend to the language that is spoken by persons under the influence of real passion, we shall find it always plain and simple; abounding indeed with those figures which express a disturbed and impetuous state of mind, such as interrogations, exclamations, and apostrophes; but never employing those which belong to the mere embellishment and parade of Speech. We never meet with any subtilty or refinement, in the sentiments of real passion. The thoughts which passion suggests, are always plain and obvious ones, arising directly from its object.[42]

Among other figures, Blair treated metaphor, allegory, hyperbole, personification, apostrophe, and exclamation. Thus what Dennis had thought of as a short list of the figures of the heart appeared as a rather long list in the works of Kames and Blair. Moreover, the new list included such figures as antithesis and metaphor, which Watts had counted among the common methods of speech.

In the latter part of the eighteenth century, then, both pragmatic and aesthetic theories of reading treated figures as important components of discourse and as having special kinds of influence on readers. However, there was a vast gulf between the two strains of theory. Where pragmatic-instrumental views of figures saw them as "common methods" of rationally signaling authorial meaning, the aestheticists saw them as "natural" expressions of "passional" feelings that naturally evoked those feelings in properly sensitized readers. Passion and emotion produced figuration and were evoked by figuration. Kames treated figures as linguistic *manifestations* of feeling; Blair stressed the capacity of figures to "delight" sensitized readers or listeners. Both men advocated a pedagogy for critical reading that aimed at sensitizing readers to *appreciate* figuration as a *manifestation* of feelings that could induce transport or reverie that delights.

The hypothesis about language that underlay Kames's and Blair's theory of reading, which in significant ways was like Sheridan's, was that a universal feature of languages is that passions evoke a class of figures, tones, looks, and gestures to which persons of taste respond passionally and unerringly. Even though Sheridan had hoped to develop a theory and pedagogy that would raise the literacy and appreciation of the populace, his hypothesis led him to an elitist theory and a pedagogy in which natural ability rather than analytic skill was central. Much the same happened to Kames and Blair.

The program for critical reading proposed by Kames and Blair also had democratic pretenses, but its starting assumptions produced a plan even less responsive to practical pedagogy and ultimately more elitist than either Burgh's or Sheridan's plan. The theory of language with which Kames and Blair worked contributed to what René Wellek has described as a "deductive, general, speculative history of poetry, which could be constructed from a knowledge of human nature, without regard to particular times or places."[43] As Wellek and Austin Warren have noted, there was the influence of "Longinus and other 'classicists' who appeal to the suffrage of all men of all times and lands," but who finally "restrict their 'all' to 'all competent judges.' "[44]

The class of competent judges to be produced by Kames's and Blair's program for critical reading were readers of refined taste. Like Dennis's reader of genius, they must come to their lessons in critical reading equipped with natural abilities that set them apart from the common run of readers. Their lessons, designed to heighten the sensitivities that already distinguished them from other readers, guided them farther and farther from rational analysis of the language of literature. The conception of language that informed this education treated verbal forms such as figures as ornaments or embellishments springing from emotion, for spontaneous translation and appreciation by a specially trained elite.

The cultural climate of the second half of the century was responsive to the allure of romanticism and primed to receive and applaud the programs of Kames and Blair. Their concept of critical reading promised to transcend mundane, rule-governed operations of what seemed the old philological mentality of classicism. The climate was right for the new criticism of aestheticism that Kames and Blair helped to create and institutionalize. The states of appreciation, transport, and reverie with which Kames and Blair associated the ultimate act of critical reading became popular goals. Yet the only pedagogical tool for helping people reach those goals was reading "the best authors." And even Kames and Blair appear to have concurred with Mason's observation that some students "can more readily enter into the Sense and Sentiments of an Author, and more easily deliver their own, than others can." The only nurture needed was to provide samples from authors with proper "Sense and Sentiments"; all else was left to nature.

There was, however, a persistent alternative to Kames's and Blair's romantic program for critical reading that had its own following. The alternative program was at odds with some of the tenets of romanticism, but it was not, as is indicated by Lowth's interest in Longinus, simply antiromantic. This program maintained some elements of classicism but undertook to *explain* them and to add new items to an account of how language and thought are related. Priestley and Campbell were intensely interested in new developments in psychology, and both believed that those developments provided further explanations and guidelines for reading and listening to discourse.

Watts had said that the common methods of speech deserved attention and analysis because they reflected the terms and structures by which minds communicate with minds. Priestley and Campbell carried out the full logic of that notion. They tried to explain *how* thought involves language and language reflects thought. Vincent Bevilacqua and Richard Murphy have stated succinctly what Priestley undertook and believed he had accomplished:

> [Priestley believed] that he had set traditional rhetorical and aesthetic subjects on a foundation of Hartleian associational psychology never before constructed. Priestley recognized that although the association of ideas plays an important role in the aesthetic theory of other English philosophers, and that he, like previous writers, sought the bases of aesthetics in the nature of the mind, in his course of lectures on rhetoric and criticism the association of ideas was not *a* principle of the mind—as in the works of Hutcheson, Gerard, and Kames—but *the* leading principle.[45]

George Campbell, too, sought to understand all communicative experience. His introduction to *The Philosophy of Rhetoric* opened with the words: "All art is founded in science." In the same essay he stated his ambition thusly:

> Our acquaintance with nature and its laws is so much extended, that we shall be enabled, in numberless cases, not only to apply to the most profitable purposes the knowledge we have thus acquired [about the mind], but to determine beforehand, with sufficient certainty, the success of every new application.[46]

And later in the same introduction Campbell wrote:

> But there is no art whatever that hath so close a connexion with all the faculties and powers of the mind, as eloquence, or the art of speaking, in the extensive sense in which I employ the term.[47]

To Campbell and Priestley all language was used instrumentally. Campbell defined "eloquence" or the art of rhetoric as follows:

> That art or talent by which the discourse is adapted to its end. All the ends of speaking are reducible to four: every speech being intended to enlighten the understanding, to please the imagination, to move the passions, or to influence the will.[48]

Priestley was equally pragmatic about how and why discourse occurs. In his second lecture he began with these words:

> All the kinds of composition may be reduced to two, viz. Narration and Argumentation. For either we propose simply to relate *facts,* with a view to communicate information, as in *History,* natural or civil, *Travels* &c. or we lay down some *proposition,* and endeavour to prove or explain it.[49]

In sum, for both men *all* use of language was purposeful and every word or combination of words was at least potentially a clue to authorial design.

This notion that all usage was or should be strategic was the foundation of Priestley's and Campbell's alternative to the formulations of Kames and Blair. Far from involving reverential suspension of rational analysis, critical reading was, to Priestley and Campbell, simply a careful and intensive extension of the rational processes of reading to comprehend. In any kind of reading or listening, said Campbell, "there are two things in every discourse which principally claim our attention, . . . the thought and the symbol by which it is communicated."[50] Attention to symbolization would, of course, entail attention to figural usage—and all other observable features of usage. Exploration of structures was, then, no mundane activity. Especially in reading critically, one was to explore all structures and other usages in order to gather the "facts" about a composition to make a judgment of it. Campbell was especially explicit on what a *critic* ought to examine: he or she was to study the merits of *usage,* to see whether the usage met tests of perspicuity, simplicity, conformity to analogous usages in the language, and agreeableness of sound. Where these tests could not yield a qualitative judgment of the work, Campbell believed "it is safest to prefer that manner which is most conformable to ancient usage."[51] Priestley devoted approximately seventy pages of *Lectures* to what he called "the bones, muscles, and nerves of a composition": the basic kinds of discussable topics and the structures of amplifying, narrating, and arguing. The rest of *Lectures,* some two hundred and sixty pages, was devoted to specific forms and usages that constituted "the covering of this body, . . . the external lineaments, the colour, the complexion, and graceful attitude of it."[52]

Campbell and Priestley treated all reading as analytical, and critical reading was simply reading in which the reader was highly informed about usage in the language in question. From Watts's notion that figural structures are especially telling clues to meaning and authorial intention there evolved a theory implying that any and all verbal choices are significant clues to intentions, expertise in communication, and the qualitative and aesthetic worth of compositions. Campbell and Priestley sought to present the *psychology* as well as an *aesthetic* of linguistic usage. Their outlook did not displace the principles of classical analysis; it supplemented and justified them by applying the principles of the mind as those principles were understood by associational psychology.

NOTES TO CHAPTER 5

1. Murray Cohen, *Sensible Words: Linguistic Practice in England, 1640–1785* (Baltimore, Md.: The Johns Hopkins University Press, 1974), p. 84.

2. Cohen, *Words,* pp. 88–89.

3. George Campbell, *The Philosophy of Rhetoric,* ed. L. Bitzer (1776; reprint Carbondale: Southern Illinois University Press, 1963), p. 149. Cohen, *Words,* p. 167 n. 23.

4. Cohen, *Words,* p. 103.

5. Cohen, *Words,* p. 104.

6. Cohen, *Words,* p. 103.

7. Norman MacLean, "From Action to Image: Theories of the Lyric in the Eighteenth Century," in *Critics and Criticism,* ed. R. S. Crane (Chicago: University of Chicago Press, 1952), p. 417.

8. Samuel Monk, *The Sublime,* 2d ed. (Ann Arbor: University of Michigan Press, 1960), pp. 82–83.

9. Hans Frei, *The Eclipse of the Biblical Narrative* (New Haven, Conn.: Yale University Press, 1974), p. 103.

10. Robert Lowth, *Isaiah. A New Translation; With a Preliminary Dissertation, and Notes Critical, Philological and Explanatory,* 2d ed. (London, 1779), pp. xxxvii–xxxix.

11. Lowth, *Preface,* p. lii.

12. Robert Lowth, *Lectures on the Sacred Poetry of the Hebrews,* trans. G. Gregory (London, 1787), p. 74.

13. Joseph Priestley, *The Rudiments of English Grammar* (1761; reprint, Menston, England: The Scolar Press, 1969), p. 46. *The Observations on Style* is a short treatise that constitutes the final section in this edition of *Rudiments.*

14. Priestley, *Rudiments,* p. 53.

15. Priestley, *Rudiments,* pp. 52–53.

16. Joseph Priestley, *A Course of Lectures on Oratory and Criticism,* ed. V. Bevilacqua and R. Murphy (1777; reprint, Carbondale: Southern Illinois University Press, 1965), p. 201.

17. Priestley, *Course,* p. 201.

18. Priestley, *Course,* p. 202.

19. Priestley, *Rudiments,* pp. 62, 46.

20. Preistley, *Course,* p. 73.

21. Priestley, *Rudiments,* pp. 57–58.

22. Priestley, *Rudiments,* p. 58.

23. Priestley, *Rudiments,* pp. 57–58.

24. George Campbell, *The Philosophy of Rhetoric,* ed. L. Bitzer (1776; reprint, Carbondale: Southern Illinois University Press, 1963), p. 263.

25. Campbell, *Philosophy,* p. 260.

26. Campbell, *Philosophy,* p. 316.

27. Campbell, *Philosophy,* p. 317.

28. Campbell, *Philosophy,* p. 317.

29. George Campbell, *The Four Gospels Translated from the Greek, with Preliminary Dissertations and Notes Critical and Explanatory* (1788; reprint, London: Tegg and Son, 1834), vol. 1, p. 7.

30. Campbell, *Gospels,* vol. 1, pp. 99–104.

31. Campbell, *Gospels,* vol. 1, p. 104.

32. Quoted in Howell, *Eighteenth-Century British Logic and Rhetoric* (Princeton, N.J.: Princeton University Press, 1971), p. 650.

33. Quoted in Howell, *Eighteenth-Century Logic,* p. 650.

34. Lord Kames, [Henry Home], *Elements of Criticism,* 8th ed. (London: Vernor and Hood, 1805), vol. 1, p. 8.

35. Monk, *Sublime,* p. 121.

36. Monk, *Sublime,* p. 115.

37. Hugh Blair, *Lectures on Rhetoric and Belles Lettres* (1783; reprint, New York: Garland, 1970), vol. 3, p. 161.

38. Kames, *Elements,* vol. 1, pp. 349–352.

39. Kames, *Elements,* vol. 2, p. 75.

40. Kames, *Elements,* vol. 1, p. 77.

41. Kames, *Elements,* vol. 2, p. 181.

42. Blair, *Lectures,* vol. 3, p. 333.

43. René Wellek, *The Rise of English Literary History* (Chapel Hill: University of North Carolina Press, 1941), p. 74.

44. René Wellek and Austin Warren, *Theory of Literature* (New York: Harcourt, Brace and World, 1956), p. 249.

45. Editors' introduction to Priestley, *Course,* p. xxii.

46. Campbell, *Philosophy,* p. xlvi.

47. Campbell, *Philosophy,* p. xlix.
48. Campbell, *Philosophy,* p. 1.
49. Priestley, *Course,* p. 6.
50. Campbell, *Philosophy,* p. 32.
51. Campbell, *Philosophy,* p. 159.
52. Priestley, *Course,* p. 72.

# 6

# IN DEFENSE OF THE
# WRITTEN LANGUAGE

During the second half of the eighteenth century, elements of a pragmatic program for critical reading were explored by writers less psychologically and philosophically oriented than Joseph Priestley and George Campbell. These writers belonged more specifically to the art-of-reading tradition than did Campbell and Priestley, and they tended to see themselves as countering the utterance notion of contextual meaning.

John Rice, William Cockin, and John Walker responded to questions about borrowings from established disciplines and about the relationships of spoken and written language with nonaesthetic and nonbelletristic answers. They agreed with Robert Lowth, Priestley, and Campbell that rhetoric properly conceived and grammar properly conceived yielded significant principles for an art of reading, and none of the three saw any need to separate reading for comprehension from critical reading. One thing that distinguished Rice, Cockin, and Walker from other writers is that they shared a sentence view of contextual meaning. Another distinction was that they argued for special values of written language, opposing Thomas Sheridan's claims for the primacy of spoken discourse. In their borrowings from rhetoric they used a conception of rhetoric that resembled that of Isaac Watts, and they, too, were interested in the nature of emphasis.

John Rice's *Introduction to the Art of Reading* was published in 1765 and served as a point of reference for the later works of William Cockin and John Walker. Rice justified his special concern with reading by commenting, "It is remarkable, that among the numerous Writers on the Arts of *Speaking* and *Writing,* there are few or none who have treated professedly on that of Reading."[1] With this claim Rice signaled his desire to disentangle the study of reading from the study of speaking and to set the two studies in a new relation to each other.

Rice proposed a hierarchy in which the study of reading, properly understood, would be the foundation for the study of speaking and training for orators. This proposal reflected a new view of the relationship between the written and the spoken forms of language. For Rice, Cockin, and Walker, study of the characteristics of written language must serve as the basis for training speakers.

Rice believed that the older association of the studies of speaking and reading had produced training that resulted in "half-reading." According to him, half-reading aimed for the general "spirit" of the author and left unattended the difficult problems of determining authorial meaning. Rice specifically identified the theory and pedagogy of half-reading with Sheridan and with programs designed primarily to train orators and actors. Rice replied, "Precepts enough have been given to qualify Players and Orators: But this is beginning at the wrong End, and is almost as bad as a Musician's attempting to teach Persons to play in Time and Tune, before they can sound simple Notes."[2] For Rice the corrective to half-reading began with the recognition that "the Art of Reading" is "the Art of converting Writing into Speech."

Cockin and Walker also proposed to reexamine assumptions about relationships between speaking and reading. Cockin, too, identified Sheridan as the major writer responsible for these mistaken views, and he added that "all our authors on the art of *reading* have imagined its principles and those of *speaking* to be the same as to delivery."[3] Cockin believed that the analogy between speaking and reading was not entirely inappropriate but had been too simply construed by his predecessors, and he proposed to reexamine the analogy in order to establish reading on its own ground.

Walker, who cited Rice's characterization of reading as "artificial speaking," agreed that there was a basis for the analogy between reading and speaking, and he proposed to reexamine the study of reading, on which the study of speaking should be based.[4] He asserted that "speaking . . . cannot be more successfully taught, than by referring us to such rules as instruct us in the art of reading."[5]

Two important beliefs informed the attempts by these three men to supplant the positions adopted by Sheridan. First, they believed that the written language was basically stable. Second, insofar as they were concerned with persons who already commanded the rudiments of linguistic usage, they saw competency in the art of reading as logically preceding competency in the art of speaking. Such positions had been suggested in the work of Priestley, with which Walker at least was familiar.

Rice objected to Sheridan's positions on several counts. He granted that the relationship between written and spoken languages was an arbitrary one, but he contended that Sheridan was mistaken when he moved from this view to the position that the written form was markedly inferior to the spoken. This led Rice to a further rejoinder, in which he objected to the pejorative tone of Sheridan's reference to written language as the "*dead Letter.*"[6] Writing had several advantages, said Rice:

> With regard to the Difference between spoken and written Language, it may, nevertheless, be not improper to observe, that the latter, having greatly the Advantage in Point of Universality, every Concession, in disputable or indifferent Cases, should be made to it by the former: In order, if possible, to effect a Conciliation of the different Dialects and provincial Modes of Utterance, common to all known Languages."[7]

The second advantage Rice discovered in written language was its "Precision": "What is spoken may be more nervous and affecting, but it is never so exact and intelligible as what is written." That a reader should treat the language on the page as a reliable guide is a conception far different from that offered by Sheridan. Rice asserted, "It is the Province of the *Reader* to unite both these Advantages, and give the Energy of the living Voice to the Precision of the dead Letter."[8] With this injunction Rice set the stage for an attempt to return the locus of contextual meaning to the printed page.

Rice's most telling attack on Sheridan and on the implications of Sheridan's theory of reading occurred in his discussion "Of the Nature and Use of Emphasis in General" and "Of the Abuse of Emphasis." The "celebrated Professor of Elocution, who lately figured in the Metropolis and Universities of Great Britain and Ireland" had, according to Rice, delivered the doctrine "that it is Emphasis which only gives Sense and Meaning to Sentences."[9] To which Rice responded, "If Emphasis only gives Sense and Meaning to Sentences, I should be glad to know of what Use is grammatical Construction."[10] He concluded:

> One might be led to imagine, by the extravagant Manner in which the Importance of Emphasis is treated by some Writers, that written Language had really no determinate Meaning at all; but that all depended upon the oral Utterance of the Reader.[11]

Rice left no doubt that a theory of reading should be grounded on a study of the written language, the stability and communicative powers of which were evident. In his succinct handling of the "Analogy between Reading and Writing" Rice found that "*Emphasis* is to the *Reading* a Language, what *Syntaxis* is to the *Writing* it; the precise Meaning of what is read or written depending respectively on *Pronunciation* or *Construction.*"[12] Rice believed that "there is a general Meaning in every Sentence grammatically written or spoken, and which must always be considered antecedent to the particular Meaning given it by Emphasis."[13] Here are elements of a sentence view of contextual meaning.

Cockin's attention to syntax was also joined to a defense of the communicative powers of the written form of language. In fact, Cockin's assertions about relationships between the written and the spoken language were even bolder than those of Rice. In stark conflict with Sheridan's position, Cockin declared that there was in use "a written language . . . so highly significant . . . that we find it does not at all require the aid of articulation."[14]

Cockin's work displayed an eighteenth-century version of a line of thought entertained today by such writers as E. D. Hirsch, Jr., and Jacques Derrida. That line of thought rejects the long-standing notion that the written language is a feebly parasitic version of the spoken language. Instead it makes the general claim that the written and the spoken languages are independent modes of communication with distinct properties that deserve study.

Cockin argued that the written and the spoken forms of language were two separate modes of communication, and he insisted that the written form had no less power and versatility than the spoken. Like Rice, whose work he acknowledged, Cockin asserted that "since in ordinary speech it is through the medium of a proper and grammatical construction of words, whose meanings are established by custom, that we convey our ideas to one another, *written language,* which professedly typifies these grammatical constructions, must, as far as bare words can extend, have every property of the *oral* one."[15] Cockin took a further step:

> Perhaps we need not stop here, but if we include what it [written language] may *suggest* as well as directly *communicate,* assert it to be in every respect as copious and significant:—That is, written language, in the same manner as speech, must have a power to affect the *fancy,* the *judgment* and the *passions.*[16]

Cockin's comment represents a complete break from Sheridan's psychological analysis of the communicative process and the alternative media of verbal communication. This break was crucial for establishing writing/reading as processes distinct from reading/speaking. If written language could, "in the same manner as speech," address "the fancy, the judgment, and the passions," its ways of doing so without the aid of "tone" and "accent" would need detailed explanations. What especially required explanation were the ways writing operated to "suggest as well as directly communicate." Cockin did not provide such explanations, but he isolated a critical problem that has not yet been clearly solved.

Cockin believed that with the burgeoning of print, the prolific use of English in its written form had given the written language a new stability and independence. Far from seeing writing as beholden to the spoken language, Cockin argued that written English was so firmly established that it could withstand the often whimsical and idiosyncratic attacks of spoken language. He wrote:

By the great quantity of books, which the art of printing has now thrown into every person's hands, we are soon acquainted with this our *mother* tongue, as it may properly be called, and become so quick and perfect in apprehending its meaning, that scarce any impediment of delivery can obstruct its passage to the understanding.[17]

He continued:

In a downright *monotony* from a whisper to plain bawling the sense is far from being obscure; all the leaps, windings, and breaks of music are unable to deface it, while the most *untoward* and *preposterous* modulation we ever meet with cannot always confound it past comprehension.[18]

Cockin did not acknowledge contemporary theoretical speculation about language. However, it is clear that Priestley's and Campbell's observations about customary use and figuration provided a theoretical perspective that lent credence to Rice's and Cockin's assertions about the suggestive powers of print and the independence of written from spoken language.

Cockin's claims for the stability of written English were, in fact, similar to assertions made earlier by Priestley. Regardless of whether Cockin borrowed from Priestley on this point, it is important to bear in mind that Cockin made a clear assertion of this stability in the latter half of the eighteenth century. E. D. Hirsch, Jr., has singled out Bradley in 1904 as having claimed that "by the beginning of the nineteenth century, the grammar of English had become permanently fixed."[19] However, a legitimate claim for English's being fixed was issued much earlier; the claim had been firmly made in the latter half of the eighteenth century.

Cockin's view of the written language as an independent and stable medium that displays grammatical construction essential to communication was perpetuated in the work of Walker. For Walker the first task of reading was grammatical analysis of the work read: "The sense of an author being the first object of reading, it will be necessary to enquire into those divisions and subdivisions of a sentence, which are employed to fix and ascertain its meaning."[20] Walker turned to Lowth's grammar for an authoritative examination of syntax in the written language.

Rice, Cockin, and Walker agreed that knowing the customary patterns of syntax—the patterns of joining words together—was essential to understanding and interpreting the meanings of written discourse. All three argued that grammatical constructions were used intentionally by authors. They believed that grammatical resources offered options among which authors chose for the purpose of communicating with others one meaning rather than another. These views considerably expanded Watts's early idea that figural constructions were chief among authorial options.

The importance of the whole of syntax in conveying meaning was explicit in Rice, even though his language shows that *oral* reading still held a strong place in his thoughts. He offered this definition: "the Art of Reading consists in *conveying* to the *Hearer the whole Meaning* of the *Writer.*" He insisted that comprehending was a fundamental part of the act of truly reading, saying, "*Reading,* as an *Art,* is not understood in that Sense, in which People may be said to *read* what they do not *comprehend.*"[21] His bias toward oral reading is apparent in the chapter "Of grammatical Construction, and the natural order of Words":

Nothing indeed is more necessary to qualify the Reader to repeat what is laid before him at Sight, and of Course to facilitate his entering into the Author's Meaning, than such a general Acquaintance with the idiomatical Modes of Expression, and the usual Arrangement of Words. It is from a Knowledge of this Arrangement that the Auditor so readily accompanies, and sometimes even anticipates the Meaning of the Speaker.[22]

It is this knowledge of "the usual Arrangement of Words" that allows access to what Rice identified as the general meaning of a sentence. In one of his attempts to counter Sheridan's claim that "Emphasis only gives Sense and Meaning to Sentences," Rice noted: "There is a general Meaning in every Sentence grammatically written or spoken, and which must always be considered antecedent to the particular Meaning given it by Emphasis."[23]

Cockin followed Rice in assigning verbal arrangement a central role in determining meaning, but in so doing he modified Rice's observations on emphasis. Cockin believed that the attention of a reader must be focused on what is shared by the written and the spoken language, on what Rice had noted as the "grammatical construction of words, whose meanings are established by custom." Cockin found that "a long acquaintance with the phraseology and construction of our language" provided the best guide to discovery of emphasis.[24] According to Cockin, emphasis "owes its rise chiefly to the *meaning* of a passage, and must therefore vary its seat according as that meaning varies."[25] By associating discovery of emphasis with a knowledge of "construction," Cockin underscored his support of Rice's objection to Sheridan's system and of Rice's criticisms of "the many instances of emphasizing given in [Sheridan's] *Lectures on Elocution*."[26]

He did not, however, follow Rice blindly. Cockin proposed an advance beyond what Rice termed "emphasis simply."[27] Cockin distinguished between two sorts of emphasis, that of sense and that of force. He thought that maintaining this distinction would counter the "too frequent and ostentatious use" of emphasis and encourage attention to emphasis of sense that "owes its rise chiefly to the meaning of the passage" read.

Emphasis of force, said Cockin, "*enforces, graces,* or *enlivens*" meanings. "Taste" allows considerable latitude in "fixing its situation and quantity."[28] But emphasis of force was "always of a magnitude inferior to that of the other species." Emphasis of sense was a more subtle matter. It involved searching out the relative significance of meanings lying beyond a single sentence. Determining emphasis of sense required determining "the meaning of a sentence with reference to something said before, presupposed by the author as general knowledge, or in order to remove an ambiguity, where a passage is capable of having more senses given to it than one."[29] With this doctrine of emphasis of sense, Cockin was clearly, if not very systematically, going beyond the sentence view of contextual meaning that Rice had offered. Almost in passing, Cockin considerably enlarged the meaning of emphasis in theory of reading.

John Walker dealt more comprehensively with the overall theory of emphasis as explored by readers. Walker noted that Cockin, "the author of the Philosophical Enquiry into the Delivery of Written Language," had provided an important advance in reading theory with his distinction between emphasis of sense and emphasis of force. However, Walker felt emphasis of sense was in need of further elaboration. Walker said few of his predecessors

> have gone farther than to tell us, that we must place the emphasis on that word in reading, which we should make emphatical in speaking; and though the importance of emphasis is insisted on with the utmost force and elegance of language, no assistance is given us to determine which is the emphatic word where several appear equally emphatical, nor have we any rule to distinguish between those words which have greater, and those which have a lesser degree of stress; the sense of the author is the sole direction we are referred to, and all is left to the taste and understanding of the reader.[30]

Accordingly Walker built a rather complicated theory of emphasis that reached from a sentence view of contextual meaning to a rhetorical view of meaning.

In *Elements of Elocution* Walker observed that the proper study of reading involves considerations of both grammar and rhetoric. He then asserted, "The sense of an author being the first object of reading, it will be necessary to enquire into those divisions and subdivisions of a sentence, which are employed to fix and ascertain its meaning: this leads us to a consideration of the doctrine of punctuation."[31] Punctuation, he said, is considered by grammar "as it clears and preserves the sense of a sentence, by combining those words together that are united in sense, and separating those which are distinct." Rhetoric considers punctuation "as it directs to such pauses, elevations, and depressions of the voice, as not only mark the sense of the sentence more precisely, but give it a variety and beauty which recommends it to the ear."[32]

Walker's treatment of punctuation used Lowth's grammar as a point of departure. *Elements* contained ninety pages displaying and examining parts of sentences and the various modes of their connections. *Rhetorical Grammar* contained ten similar lessons. In each of these sections, Walker found it necessary to "enquire into the nature of a sentence, and to distinguish it into its different kinds" before examining the variety of typical relationships among and connections between members. This elaborate examination of the common methods of joining words provided the body of material from which Walker derived what he considered his new contribution to a theory of emphasis.

A grammatical view of sentences and an analysis of the various syntactic patterns through which sense is displayed together formed the foundation for Walker's discussions of force and emphasis. Grammatical analysis helps a reader employ Walker's two categories of force, which he contrasted with Cockin's single concept of force. Grammatical analysis assists a reader in understanding the category of force that includes "the conjunctions, particles, and words understood, which are obscurely and feebly pronounced." It also aids a reader in understanding the category of force that includes "the substantives, verbs and more significant words, which are firmly and distinctly pronounced." As Walker saw it, grammatical analysis of both minimally forceful words (e.g., conjunctions and particles) and potentially emphatic terms (e.g., substantives and verbs) was necessary in order for a reader to distinguish clearly among the patterns of force implied by a text.

This procedure alone was not enough, however. Walker turned from the two categories of force to the category of emphasis associated with those words he referred to as having "a peculiarity of meaning." At this point he contended that grammatical analysis of sentences needed to be supplemented by, but not supplanted by, rhetorical analysis. He gave special attention to two traditional rhetorical figures: antithesis and ellipsis. Why these? Walker offered the following generalization about antithesis: "The principal circumstance that distinguishes emphatical words from others, seems to be a meaning which points out, or distinguishes, something as distinct or opposite to some other thing. When this opposition is expressed in words, it forms an antithesis, the opposite parts of which are always emphatical."[33] Walker was here addressing a question long latent in discussions of the art of reading: How is it that the "peculiar sense" of one or two words arises from their dependence on the words with which they are joined in context? His statement makes clear that in his view peculiar sense, or peculiarity of meaning, arises from rhetorical usage, as distinct from grammatical construction. He reinforced this point elsewhere in his writings.

Walker's definition of emphasis in *Rhetorical Grammar* was much like that in *Elements of Elocution*. In *Rhetorical Grammar* Walker asked, "Now what is this peculiar meaning in words, which . . . properly denominates them emphatical?" He answered, "This question, however difficult it may appear at first sight, may be answered in one word, *opposition*. Whenever words are contrasted *with*, contradistinguished *from,* or opposed *to,* other words, they are always emphatical." Walker then divided opposition into expressed or overt opposition and implied or "elliptical" opposition.[34]

Attempting to offer a more practical pedagogy, Walker formed what he considered a master pedagogical tool. Walker was the first, in the tradition of the art of reading English and in the tradition of critical reading, to claim that the oppositional structure of antithesis alone describes the relationships in which a key word or words come to be emphatic. Watts and later writers had offered examples of expressed antithesis in their discussions of emphasis, and Watts had given prominence to the role of antithesis in conveying meaning as he treated "foils." Rice, too, had suggested the importance of antithesis in his comments on "The Antithesis . . . marked by Pronunciation." But none had made Walker's general claim.

Walker believed that in cases of expressed or overt opposition "where both parts of the antithesis are laid down, and the opposition appears at full length," a reader familiar with the customary patterns of joining words and dividing sentences and familiar with the means of indicating the patterns and divisions through utterance (one who has mastered the first thirty-one lessons of *Rhetorical Grammar*) will have little problem determining and conveying the meaning.

However, matters were quite otherwise in cases of elliptical or implied opposition. Walker noted, "The greatest difficulty in reading, lies in a discovery of those words which are in opposition to something not expressed, but understood."[35] Here Walker drew into his system an aspect of contextual meaning treated by Cockin as the "pre-understood." Walker discerned two distinct manifestations of opposition that can occur when something expressed is antithetical to something understood. The first sort he described as "evident" though not expressed. One example he used came from Pope:

Get wealth and place, if possible with grace,
If not by any means get wealth and place.

Here it appears evidently, that the words *any means,* which are the most emphatical, are directly opposed to the means understood by the word *grace,* and the last line is perfectly equivalent to this. "If not by these means, by any other means, get wealth and place."[36]

As he moved to the less-evident manifestations of elliptical opposition, Walker discussed ellipsis and the procedures a reader should employ in dealing with it. In these discussions he used a concept that closely corresponded to Rice's notion of general meaning. To deal with the less evident manifestations of elliptical opposition, said Walker, "we must have recourse to the general import of the sentence; and whatever word we suppose to be emphatical, must be tried, by pronouncing it more forcibly than the rest of the words; and if this pronunciation suggests a phrase, which, if inserted in the sentence, would explain and illustrate it, we may be sure that word is emphatical." Walker provided the following example and discussion:

And if each system in gradation roll,
Alike essential to th' amazing whole;
The least confusion but in ONE, not all
That system only, but the whole must fall.

In the third line of this passage, we find an uncommon effort in the author to express "the strong connexions, nice dependencies" of one part of the general system upon another: and if we lay a strong emphasis on the word *one,* we shall find this connexion and dependency very powerfully enforced; for it will suggest this antithesis: "the least confusion, not in several or a great many parts of the universe, but even in one, would bring confusion on the whole." This paraphrase we not only find consistent with the sense of the poet, but greatly illustrative of it; and hence we may determine the word *one* to be emphatical.[37]

In further discussion of less-evident elliptical oppositions, Walker characterized the necessary activity of a reader as an "unfolding and displaying" or "drawing out the signification of emphatic words." Describing the paraphrastic process as exemplified by the lines just quoted, Walker said, "This drawing out the signification of emphatic words, seems the best guide in cases where the sense is not quite obvious, and will lead us to decide in many doubtful cases, where nothing but the taste of the reader is commonly appealed to."[38]

Walker was justified in claiming that he had provided a more useful pedagogical tool than his predecessors' directions for determining emphasis. He was also justified in suggesting that some of his predecessors had offered approaches to emphasis that relied too heavily on the reader's taste. His corrective to an overreliance on taste underscores a parallel between his program for basic reading and Lowth's, Priestley's, and Campbell's program for critical reading. For Walker a fundamental task of the reader was careful examination of structures through which meaning, far from being reducible to individual words treated as mere signs, comes to be conveyed.

The procedures advocated by Walker were forerunners of techniques employed by such twentieth-century reading theorists as Gérard Genette, who also explores relationships between rhetorical and grammatical concerns. Johnathan Culler has noted that for a student using Genette's techniques, "the rhetorical figures with which he is familiar define a series of operations" to be performed on texts. The perspective of Genette, and of Walker before him, allows one "to think of training in rhetoric as a way of providing the student with a set of formal models which he can use in interpreting literary works."[39]

Walker's merging of the grammatical concerns about syntax with rhetorical concerns about the structure of two rhetorical figures revitalized in the late eighteenth century two staples of Watts's early conception of reading: the rhetorical view of emphasis and the belief that the structures of at least some figures are trustworthy common methods of speech that "suggest" or give clues to the sense and force of what is written. There is even some continuity of interest in rhetorical and grammatical considerations in a stream of thought that runs from the Renaissance to the late eighteenth century. The explorations by Renaissance scholars of interdependent grammatical and rhetorical considerations for understanding syntax were acknowledged by those who fostered a new grammatical tradition in England early in the eighteenth century. And there are relationships between these early-eighteenth-century concerns and certain modern work that has been influenced by the studies of Roman Jakobson. Walker in particular, but also Rice and Cockin, were important contributors to this line of thought because they insisted that both grammatical and rhetorical considerations needed to be taken into account in order to understand a text. What Walker, Rice, and Cockin added to the early Renaissance interests was the notion that rhetorical considerations must *supplement* grammatical considerations, not just in the study of syntax, but in order to stipulate how a reader can understand entire texts.

More remains to be said about Walker's treatment of rhetorical figures. His handling of emphasis through the structures of antithesis and ellipsis shows his intention to ground reading theory on the older conception of rhetorical emphasis. It seemed to him that rhetorical emphasis, with its patterns through which an author calls attention to or sets off some parts of a discourse from others, was the foundation of linguistic emphasis, with its patterns of stress in oral utterance. Walker recognized that rhetorical emphasis is often a function of rhetorical figures, and he extended his coverage of figures beyond antithesis and ellipsis, though with little comment. He divided figures into two types, those "common to every species of composition" and those which "belong more particularly to oratory." He included in the former category metaphor, allegory, metonymy, synechdoche, hyperbole, and catechresis. The figures in this category, which he labeled "rhetorical," "have no reference to delivery, and may be considered as perfect, whether they are spoken or not."[40] In the latter category Walker placed figures such as irony, aposiopesis, and climax. He said of these "oratorical" figures that they "suppose a pronunciation suitable to each, and without which they have not half their beauty."[41]

A major motivation for Walker, Rice, and Cockin was to undermine what they took to be Thomas Sheridan's misperceptions. Sheridan had severely downgraded the written form of communication, whereas Walker, Rice, and Cockin saw writing as freighted with clues to authorial meanings. Sheridan's epistemological assumptions and his conceptions of the primacy and richness of speech and the feebleness of writing led him to suppose that there must always be lapses of communication between authors and their readers. In his view those lapses could only be corrected through the reader's resort to oral delivery expressing linguistic emphasis. Rice, Cockin, and especially Walker flatly disagreed. They insisted that authorial design and rhetorical emphasis could be discovered by following clues provided by printed texts. Walker, for example, granted that experimenting with oral delivery might aid a reader's understanding, but he did not believe that testing out meanings orally was essential in the most serious reading. By expanding the views of figurative language earlier offered by Watts, Lowth, Priestley, and Campbell, Walker directly contradicted Sheridan's analyses by insisting that the most crucial communicative figures were fully available to writers and fully discoverable from the structuration of texts.

## THE TRADITION OF RHETORICAL GRAMMAR

Nowhere was the contrast between the theories of Sheridan and Walker more evident than in their treatments of "rhetorical grammar." Walker's, and also Rice's, understanding of rhetorical grammar was distinctly different from Sheridan's because Walker and a few others explicitly denied that the written form of language was inferior to the spoken.

There were four significant contributions to a short-lived "tradition" of teaching rhetorical grammar in the second half of the eighteenth century. Each offered students of reading and speaking a rhetorical view of discourse as a supplement to a grammatical view. One was John Rice's statement of a plan for a rhetorical grammar. Another was William Kenrick's enactment of Rice's plan without acknowledging Rice but with extensive, verbatim borrowings from Rice's *The Art of Reading*. Another was Sheridan's *Rhetorical Grammar,* the second section of which was "On Public Speaking." It was probably the publisher's, not Sheridan's, decision to include that section, which was an unacknowledged selection out of James Burgh's *Art of Speaking*. The last contribution was John Walker's *Rhetorical Grammar*.

In an appendix to *The Art of Reading,* John Rice offered the "sketch of a plan" for a forthcoming *Rhetorical Grammar* and a companion *Rhetorical Dictionary*. ("The *Grammar* in one Vol. *Octavo*. To be published as soon as possible. The *Dictionary* in one Vol. *Quarto*. To be published at the latest before the end of next Winter.")[42] For whatever reasons, Rice did not bring his plan to print. Considerable mystery surrounds the fact that a work clearly designed as the execution of Rice's plan was published (with no acknowledgment of Rice) in 1773 by William Kenrick, to whom Rice had dedicated *The Art of Reading*. Kenrick made some modifications of Rice; however, the skeleton of his work, and much of its flesh and spirit, were taken from the appendix to *The Art of Reading*.

Kenrick's *Rhetorical Grammar* was originally published in 1773 as a preface to his *New Dictionary of the English Tongue*. The *Rhetorical Grammar* was then issued as an independent publication in 1774. In his introduction Kenrick referred to both the grammar and the dictionary and wrote that since their "original proprietor," Jacob Tonson, had died, "I have been induced, in justice to his assigns, to publish in my own name, what was projected chiefly for the emolument of another."[43] That "another" referred to John Rice, from whose work Kenrick borrowed so liberally and whose *Art of Reading,* with its plan for a rhetorical grammar and dictionary, had been published by Tonson.

In keeping with Rice's plan, and unlike Sheridan's *Rhetorical Grammar,* the work offered under Kenrick's name undertook to demonstrate an oral reader's extensive dependence on trustworthy characteristics of written language. Given Kenrick's massive borrowings from Rice, it is not surprising that his *Rhetorical Grammar* reflected Rice's view of the relationship between the printed text and the oral utterance of a reader.

One section of Kenrick's grammar—"Of the Composition of Sentences, and their Delivery in common and oratorical Discourse"—was a discussion of the connections between the two kinds of language.

Kenrick, following Rice, said it was necessary to attend to the customary, "idiomatical order of expression" as displayed in the written language.[44] A great deal of this section was a literal restatement of passages from Rice's *The Art of Reading,* including the distinction between "natural" and "customary" order:

> Much has been written, to little purpose, about the natural order or succession of words in discourse; but, as languages were not originally formed on philosophical principles, their grammar and idiom are of course widely different. It is indeed generally imagined that, in ordinary discourse our words follow each other in some *natural* order: but on due examination perhaps we ought to say *habitual,* instead of *natural.*[45]

Kenrick also included Rice's observation:

> Nothing indeed is more necessary to qualify a reader to repeat what is laid before him at sight, and of course to facilitate his entering into an author's meaning, than such a general acquaintance with the idiomatical modes of expression, and the usual arrangement of words.[46]

To this was appended Rice's discussion of the distinction between general and particular meaning.[47]

The notion of a distinction between "common and oratorical discourse" was central to the relationship between grammar and rhetoric as set forth in the *Rhetorical Grammar* attributed to Kenrick. There, as in Rice's *Art of Reading,* the fundamental concern of a reader in determining authorial meaning was the "grammatical construction" of sentences. The reader was directed to "consider first the simple meaning of each sentence, according to its grammatical construction, and as it stands detached from every other part." The basic grammatical knowledge a reader needed was, in Rice's terms, "the idiomatical order of words, and all the allowed modes of transposition."

After carefully considering individual sentences grammatically, a reader was to turn to rhetorical considerations. In this activity the reader would examine the relations of each sentence "and the relation of all its parts to the context." The search for the seat of oratorical or rhetorical emphasis was to be made while remembering that "the emphasis should ever be consistent with grammatical construction, and should serve to confirm and enforce the meaning of each particular sentence, while it connects and gives greater significancy and pathos to the whole."

The *Rhetorical Grammar* attempted to supplement what Rice had provided in *The Art of Reading*. One of the most significant hopes expressed by Kenrick was that the supplement would lead students beyond the treatment of sentences in isolation to a consideration of sentences joined in the discourse as a whole. However, this hope was not realized, for he did not advance the theory of handling sentences joined beyond the suggestive lines of thought contained in the passages I have quoted. However, some further advance occurred in the work of Walker, which I discuss after contrasting Sheridan's *Rhetorical Grammar* to the writings of Rice and Kenrick.

The material for the body of Sheridan's *Rhetorical Grammar* (1781) had been published as the introduction to Sheridan's *General Dictionary* in 1780 and was largely taken from, and was in keeping with, his *Course of Lectures*. His handling of accent and emphasis in *Rhetorical Grammar* was the same as that in the earlier work. In treating "pauses or Stops," for example, he reiterated the positions that had elicited reactions from Rice and Cockin that I have already discussed:

> The truth is, the modern art of punctuation was not taken from the art of speaking, which certainly ought to have been its archetype, and probably would, had that art been studied and brought to perfection by the moderns; but was in great measure regulated by the rules of grammar, which they had studied; that is, certain parts of speech are kept together, and others divided by stops, according to their grammatical construction, often without reference to the pauses used in discourse. And the only general rule, by which pauses can be regulated properly, has been either unknown, or unattended to; which is, that pauses, for the most part, depend on emphasis.

He repeated his claim that "emphasis is the link which connects words together, and forms them into sentences, or into members of sentences."[48]

Sheridan's *Rhetorical Grammar* moved from pronunciation of "simple sounds" through "rules for the pronunciation of English words" to culminate in the section "Of the Art of Delivery." Subjects taken up in the last section were articulation, accent, pronunciation, emphasis, pauses or stops, pitch or management of voice, tones, and recitation of poetic numbers. The supplement, which was a selection from Burgh's *Art of Speaking*, included Burgh's extensive discussion of the principal passions "and their modes of expression." Thus Sheridan's *Rhetorical Grammar* with the section from Burgh stood as a perpetuation of his and Burgh's defense of the spoken form of language considered as distinct from and far more valuable than the written form of language.

Walker's *Rhetorical Grammar* also contained borrowings from and condensations of his earlier views. However, unlike Sheridan's, Walker's *Rhetorical Grammar* contained a large body of new material that reflected a rhetorical view of literature, which Walker considered an essential addition. Such a view, Walker believed, significantly augmented what the grammatical view of discourse could supply to a reader's understanding. In it Walker treated the figures, again divided into rhetorical and oratorical categories. Walker was actually elaborating his fundamental position that a grammatical view of syntax or words joined (fully available to the written form of language) must be linked with a rhetorical view in order to reveal the functions of rhetorical figures also fully available to the written form of language. Walker had thus outlined the full coverage of a grammatical-linguistic-rhetorical conception of the art of reading.

Most of the writers discussed in this and the preceding chapter contributed to the evolution of that conception. Through Rice, Cockin, and especially Walker, a tradition stressing that reading is an *art* was supplied with a *method* of reading and a *plan* for instruction in reading. The method and plan contained essential principles of critical reading that had been offered by Lowth, Priestley, and Campbell. Some of Watts's concerns and motivations early in the century also informed these later authors, whether or not they deliberately looked to Watts for guidance.

In view of the controversies I have reviewed, it is especially important to note that Rice, Cockin, and Walker conceived of reading as a *single art* that could yield both *comprehension* and *judgment*. The art they conceived could have such broad results because it entailed rhetorical as well as grammatical and linguistic considerations. The rhetorical considerations were largely those that had to do with figuration; figures and tropes were looked upon as common methods of speech and as relatively standard *strategic* ways of conveying meanings to readers in any language. The reading theorists I have discussed did not carry their interests in classical *dispositio* beyond sentences and their interrelationships, but they did recognize "the whole discourse" as a context for its meaningful elements even though they gave only partial advice on how to look for meanings in the ways sentences were joined together. The art of reading, these writers argued, consisted of applying to texts customarily used grammatical, linguistic, and rhetorical principles for the purpose of finding the meanings authors intentionally embedded in their discourses.

The art of reading urged and taught by Rice, Cockin, and especially Walker was like the methods of critical reading proposed by others: it was an analytical, intellectual art, but it asserted no need to separate reading for comprehension from critical reading. Readers would bring different natural abilities to their task, but the newly evolved theory implied that anyone could acquire knowledge of the English language and of the idiomatic, rhetorical options open to writers. Once so instructed, all readers would read with greater understanding—whether they read silently or orally.

Walker asserted that the art of reading involved understanding sentences' relationships to one another, as well as understanding how words interrelated within single sentences. While his treatment of figuration advanced the art of reading, neither he nor his contemporaries fully explored how sentences were to be studied for their relationships. The art therefore remained in a sentence-view stage. Even so, the Rice-Cockin-Walker doctrines were, and were meant to be, directly opposed to theories of reading that rested heavily on such difficult-to-teach concepts as natural ability, genius, and searching for ideas above their expressions. Walker in particular opposed such theories by insisting that grammatical principles and figural analysis were teachable and could be profitably applied in any kind of reading. Behind this contention lay another of equal significance: for readers and writers, at least, the written form of language is a primary form of communication offering a wide range of resources that can be used strategically by writers and are open to systematic analysis and interpretation by readers.

NOTES TO CHAPTER 6

1. John Rice, *An Introduction to the Art of Reading* (1765; reprint, Menston, England: The Scolar Press, 1969), p. 1.
2. Rice, *Reading,* p. 9.
3. William Cockin, *The Art of Delivering Written Language* (1775; reprint, Menston, England: The Scolar Press, 1969), p. 18.
4. John Walker, *A Rhetorical Grammar* (1785; reprint, Menston, England: The Scolar Press, 1971), p. 29.
5. John Walker, *Elements of Elocution* (1781; reprint, Menston, England: The Scolar Press, 1969), vol. 1, p. 2.
6. Rice, *Reading,* p. 194.
7. Rice, *Reading,* p. 195.
8. Rice, *Reading,* p. 195.
9. Rice, *Reading,* p. 202.
10. Rice, *Reading,* p. 208.
11. Rice, *Reading,* p. 235.

12. Rice, *Reading,* p. 6.
13. Rice, *Reading,* p. 208.
14. Cockin, *Art,* p. 131.
15. Cockin, *Art,* p. 127.
16. Cockin, *Art,* pp. 127–28.
17. Cockin, *Art,* p. 130.
18. Cockin, *Art,* pp. 130–31.
19. E. D. Hirsch, Jr., *The Philosophy of Composition* (Chicago: University of Chicago Press, 1977), pp. 36ff.
20. Walker, *Elements,* vol. 1, p. 3.
21. Rice, *Reading,* p. 2.
22. Rice, *Reading,* pp. 359–60.
23. Rice, *Reading,* p. 208.
24. Cockin, *Art,* p. 42.
25. Cockin, *Art,* p. 33.
26. Cockin, *Art,* p. 37.
27. Cockin, *Art,* p. 36.
28. Cockin, *Art,* p. 41.
29. Cockin, *Art,* p. 36.
30. Walker, *Elements,* vol. 2, pp. 16–17.
31. Walker, *Elements,* vol. 1, p. 3.
32. Walker, *Elements,* vol. 1, p. 3.
33. Walker, *Elements,* vol. 2, p. 27.
34. Walker, *Grammar,* pp. 101–2.
35. Walker, *Elements,* vol. 2, p. 33.
36. Walker, *Elements,* vol. 2, p. 28.
37. Walker, *Grammar,* p. 103.
38. Walker, *Elements,* vol. 2, p. 83.
39. Johnathan Culler, *Structuralist Poetics* (Ithaca, N.Y.: Cornell University Press, 1975), p. 179.
40. Walker, *Grammar,* p. 136.
41. Walker, *Grammar,* p. 136.
42. Rice, *Reading,* p. 308.
43. William Kenrick, *A Rhetorical Grammar of the English Language* (1784; reprint, Menston, England: The Scolar Press, 1972), p. v.
44. Kenrick, *Grammar,* p. 31.
45. Kenrick, *Grammar,* pp. 27–28.
46. Kenrick, *Grammar,* p. 30.
47. Kenrick, *Grammar,* pp. 33–34.
48. Sheridan, *Grammar,* p. 103.

# 7

# THE PRAGMATICS OF READING

A prominent theme in what became the dominant eighteenth-century theory of reading was that the structures of rhetorical figures and tropes needed special study by astute readers. This notion was furthered in the nineteenth century by a theorist who is now little known, Benjamin Smart, a prolific writer on grammar, logic, rhetoric, and "sematology."

Between 1810 and 1842, as "Professor of Elocution and Reader of Shakespeare," Smart published the following works: *Practical Logic: or Hints to Theme Writers; A Grammar of English Pronunciation; The Practice of Elocution; The Theory of Elocution, Exhibited in Connexion with a New and Philosophical Account of the Nature of Instituted Language; A New Pronouncing Dictionary of the English Language (Walker Remodeled); An Outline of Sematology, or an Essay Towards Establishing a New Theory of Grammar, Logic, and Rhetoric; Sequel to Sematology; and A Way Out of Metaphysics.*

Smart's writings reflect his extensive knowledge of his British contemporaries' speculations about language, and his work indicates his willingness to enter into the central disputes of the new century. In October 1817, before the Philosophical Society of London, Smart delivered a paper that was later reworked to form the introduction to *The Theory of Elocution*. In that publication Smart discussed his desire to explore theory of language in relation to the study of reading. Noting that *The Practical Grammar* he had published in 1810 had promised a future treatise on "the higher requisites of Delivery," Smart spoke of the period between 1810 and 1817 as one in which he was preoccupied by the belief that "there was something deficient in all the Theories to which the practice of Elocution is referred."[1] In *The Theory of Elocution* Smart offered what he believed to be a new and stronger foundation on which to assemble the constructive studies of his predecessors to produce a complete art of reading.

Smart was attracted particularly to the work of John Walker. He observed that Walker had "given rules founded on theoretical views that apply to a certain extent, but which seem to want the support of a system."[2] The theoretical views that produced pedagogical results to which Smart largely subscribed were those in which Walker insisted on the importance of a reader's attending to words joined in discourse and on the relevance of the structures of rhetorical figures and tropes to an understanding of the structure of language. These were views associated with the impulse to move beyond the Lockean notion that the word, as the sign for an idea, is the unit of meaning. Smart believed that his predecessors had advanced toward, but had stopped short of, a radical theoretical alternative to Lockean thought about meaning, similar to one explored by Dugald Stewart.

Smart contended that to understand the instrumental character of language properly, one must greatly revise customary thought about each of the three parts of the trivium: grammar, logic, and rhetoric. In *The Theory of Elocution,* and in his discussion of grammar in *An Outline of Sematology,* Smart provided the rudiments of what I term his "instrumental theory" of contextual meaning. Having defined "sematology" as *the doctrine of signs* showing how the mind operates by their means in obtaining . . . knowledge," Smart examined artificial or instituted language as a "necessary instrument" of the mind.[3]

Smart's treatment of sematology signaled the emergence of a very modern point of view—only hinted at by some of Smart's predecessors in pragmatic theory—that an understanding of how language works must be the foundation on which theories of epistemology and psychology are constructed. Similarly, some moderns, among them Paul de Man, have recently reasserted the priority of coming to terms with language as the basis for understanding the workings of the mind.

Smart was explicit about the theory of language he wished to overturn: "It may not, perhaps, be anywhere formally stated, yet the common opinion of language seems to be, that every separate word is the sign of a different idea, and that the progress and order of our words in speaking, represents a similar progression and order in our thoughts."[4] This assumption had been perpetuated in the handling of the parts of speech and by "the definitions and general reasoning in Grammar," he wrote.[5] "Now instead of taking it for granted . . . that men sat down to invent the parts of speech, because they found they had ideas which respectively required them, we assert that men have originally no such ideas as correspond to the parts of speech."[6]

On such subjects as the nature of reading, the relationships between the study of oral reading and the study of speaking, and the relationships between spoken and written forms of language, Smart's conceptions strongly resembled those of John Rice, William Cockin, and especially Walker. Smart, however, asserted more emphatically than his predecessors that writing is the original and primary language for all forms of reading. Even for an oral reader the nature of written language is the *first* consideration. Said Smart in *The Theory of Elocution*: "Exercise for improvement in the art of Oral Delivery can scarcely be conducted with advantage, but by having recourse to written language; and instruction in Elocution, (as modern usage employs the term,) is therefore the same with instruction in Reading." Here was a firm claim that for reading, at least, writing is the original and primary language.

Smart's theory of language was linked with a view of epistemology similar to that expressed in the work of Isaac Watts and George Campbell. Influenced by Stewart, Smart accepted the Scottish Common Sense Movement's modification of Lockean epistemology that proposed that the mind has the capacity to achieve abstractions "by acts of comparison and judgment upon its passively received ideas."

By the time of Smart's writing, this common-sense epistemology had, in the work of such writers as Campbell and Stewart, developed with a parallel theory of language. That theory made use of Campbell's insights into the close association of thought and language and the necessity of attending to the multiple methods by which words are joined in discourse, including methods associated with rhetorical figures. Smart wanted to develop this theory of language further and to ground theory and pedagogy of reading firmly on it.

Smart's instrumental view of contextual meaning resembled Campbell's and Stewart's conceptions of language, and it also was strikingly similar to some twentieth-century conceptions of language, including the theory of contextual meaning proposed by I. A. Richards in *Philosophy of Rhetoric*. Smart believed that language was a "necessary effect of reason, as well as its necessary instrument." As he elaborated this view, he commented on an original principle of language, observed the instrumentality of language in the process of thought, and discussed the instrumentality of language in the process of communication. Smart contended that "the earliest sounds which children utter, the earliest sounds which would be employed in the first utterances of a language, are virtual sentences." He hypothesized that in the primitive employment of "virtual sentences," "it eventually became impossible to find a new sign for every occasion," and it became necessary to employ "an expedient" derived from the fundamental "capacity for abstraction." This notion of the "expedient" was a prominent and vital feature of Smart's theory of language and the theory of reading he based on it. Smart said, "The expedient is nothing more than this:—when a new expression is wanted, two or more signs [virtual sentences], each of which has served a particular purpose, are put together in such a manner as to modify each other, and thus, in their *united* capacity, to answer the new particular purpose in view."[7]

With this notion of the expedient, Smart was extending the familiar figuration theme into new theoretical territory that theorists and critics more than a century later explored in detail. Smart believed that the means of joining two or more familiar signs to render new meaning were catalogued in the traditional lists of figures and tropes. Here he was articulating the basic premise of explorations such as that Richards developed when he treated metaphor as a master trope of interinanimation, as Kenneth Burke fleshed out in his study of four master tropes, and as Roman Jakobson developed in his studies of metaphoric and metonymic thinking. Smart did not anticipate these modern studies, but the historical record should show that it was Smart, now almost forgotten, who isolated the combinational principle that the later studies developed in detail.

When he discussed the role of language in ongoing thought, Smart said that when virtual sentences or signs are combined with other virtual sentences or signs, they achieve in combination the status of separate words. But, he reminded his readers, "The separate words . . . do not stand for passively received ideas, but for abstract notions."[8] He believed that Locke's "wide use of the word *idea* has been a cause of the widest confusion in other writers," and he insisted that each separately viewed word of a sentence "is not the sign of any idea whatever which the mind passively receives, but of an abstraction which reason obtains by acts of comparison and judgment upon its passively-received ideas."[9] Thus individual words are not, as Locke had conceived them, meaningful as individual units standing for individual ideas. Instead they are meaningful as records of past mental actions performed by means of, and within the guidelines of, linguistic expedients. Here Smart foreshadowed some of the lines of thought found in the work of Richards, in the later work of Ludwig Wittgenstein, and in "speech act theory." Smart was clearly working in the direction of modern attempts to displace the dictionary mentality that finds words meaningful by virtue of the ideas they contain and to trace meanings by exploring "use" and the rules governing the acts performed in and through language.

Observing that "in our theory of language, every word was once a sentence, Smart said that words treated individually are "the signs of knowledge obtained by antecedent acts of judgment, and deposited in the mind; which signs are fitted to be the means of reaching further knowledge."[10] In the sentence "John walks," "the separate meaning of the word *walks,* is a knowledge that another may walk as well as John." Thus as a sign of knowledge obtained by past acts of comparison and judgment, "properly called a notion not an idea," the virtual sentence "walks" exists as a record or "abbreviation" of past sentences in which the term has been used.[11]

Smart further stressed that all words, even those traditionally treated as signs of simple ideas, are, considered individually, "abstract or general." He said:

> This is as true of such words as yellow, white, heat, cold, soft, hard, bitter, sweet, and the like signs of what Locke calls simple ideas as of any other: for we can evidently use these words on an infinity of different occasions; and the power of so using them is an effect and a proof of our *knowing* that the different occasions on which we use the same word, have a something in common, or in some way resemble.[12]

Smart made the forward-looking comment that "it surely will not be contended that any one knows the meaning of a word beyond the cases to which we can apply it."[13] Here, too, Smart was presaging a more modern "use" perspective on the operations of language.

In discussing the process by which a speaker or writer "spells" a thought, Smart asserted that "we are mistaken if we suppose that every word in a sentence signifies a part of the whole thought, and that the progression of the words is in correspondence with a progression of ideas which the mind first puts together within, and then signifies without." Instead, according to Smart, the process ought to be described as one in which a speaker or writer *forces* individual words to relinquish their general or abstract meaning. He believed that

> while all words . . . acquire an abstract or general meaning, every communication which we purpose to make by their means, must, in comparison with their separate signification, be particular; and our putting them together in order to form a sign for the more particular thought, will be to deprive them of the abstract or general meaning which they had individually.[14]

At this point Smart's theory foreshadowed Richards's belief that "meanings, from the very beginning, have a primordial generality and abstractness."[15] With his notion of words as virtual sentences, and with the relationship he posited between general or abstract meanings and particular meanings, Smart was elevating earlier concerns identified by Joseph Priestley's, Cockin's, and Walker's interest in ellipsis. In Smart's treatment, ellipsis was given the status of a primary principle of meaning. In doing so Smart indicated, far more clearly than had any of his predecessors, the need for the kinds of explorations begun in twentieth-century efforts to understand the roles and structures of the unsaid in reading.

Smart moved well beyond his predecessors when he said that the process of depriving individual words of their general meanings for the sake of giving them particular meanings is never completed until the whole discourse is completed: "[until the] sentence or oration is completed the Word is unsaid which represents the speaker's thought." Smart had departed so far from key-word views and sentence views of contextual meaning that he could say: "the words of a sentence, understood in their separate capacity, do not constitute the meaning of the whole sentence, . . . [for] they are not by themselves significant; . . . they are significant only as the instrumental means for getting at the meaning of the . . . whole sentence or the whole discourse."[16] "The parts that make up the whole expression," he said, "are parts of the expression in the same manner as syllables are parts of a word, but are *not* parts of the one whole meaning in any other way than as the instrumental means for reaching and for communicating that meaning."[17] Smart's vision of the interactions of words joined was most specifically expressed when he said that as soon as two individual words are joined, they begin to "limit and determine each other."[18] Smart used that same postulate in explaining all verbal interplay: virtual sentences, sentences, and whole discourses "limit and determine" their parts.

Among Smart's predecessors in the pragmatic strain of reading theory, Watts had recognized that his view of figures as strategic instrumentalities had implications for a broader view of method, arrangement, or *dispositio,* but his key-word view of contextual meaning prevented him from elaborating those implications. Smart's instrumental view, however, cleared the way for a conception of figures as large-scale structures that constituted the whole of method, arrangement, or *dispositio.* The expedients, the rhetorical figures and tropes intertwined throughout a discourse, created what Smart referred to as the "particular" meanings of each individual piece of discourse. A completed discourse, Smart said, "is as completely indivisible with respect to the meaning conveyed by it as a whole, as is a word which consists only of a single syllable, or a single sound."[19] Smart had arrived at a view of meaning that Richards much later called an "interinanimation" view, according to which the meanings of individual words depend upon "the other words before and after them in the sentence."[20] Indeed, Smart went further than Richards: he contended that *all* terms in a discourse "interinanimate" all others.

Clearly, in probing the implications of his instrumental view of contextual meaning, Smart advanced reading theory and pedagogy on several fronts. One of those fronts had to do with readers' searches for authorial intent. Having moved far beyond his predecessors' key-word and sentence views, Smart portrayed a more complicated act of reading. The reader must not lapse into the erroneous belief that any parts of the discourse (key words, topic sentences, and the like) are isolable for determining authorial intent. What the reader pursues, guided by the tropological expedients of language, is the thought of the writer, and that thought will be no less complex than the interinanimated meanings of the entire discourse.

Smart further complicated his predecessors' notions by reevaluating traditional concepts of language. In discussing language as an instrument of communication, Smart asserted that

> as a rhetorical instrument, language is, in truth, much more used to explore the minds of those who are addressed, than to represent, by an expression of correspondent unity, the thought of the speaker;—rather to put other minds into a certain posture or train of thinking, than pretending to convey at once what the speaker thinks.[21]

With this observation, Smart went far beyond his predecessors in defining what constituted "rhetoric properly conceived." Under his definition, discourse was always *adaptive* and always motivated by at least some degree of persuasive intent. Moreover, discourse could never be totally *expressive* because of "how little one mind can directly represent or open itself to another."[22] The expedients of language permitted a writer or speaker to adapt communication to the "knowledge the hearers have already attained, or to feelings they have already experienced, in order to conduct them to some discovery he wishes them to make, or to some unexperienced train of thought conducive to such discovery."[23] Without saying so, Smart had recaptured an essentially Aristotelian view of enthymematic communication. He was asking readers (and listeners) to supply the unsaid, to assume that adaptive persuasiveness was part of each author's intent, and to recognize and accept the fact that language is an imperfect vehicle for self-disclosure. But Smart was not teaching that communication is necessarily "deceptive" because of its intentionality and the limitations of linguistic media.

As had Priestley, Smart rejected the view in which "the various tropes and figures of which [a] discourse is made up, are apt to be looked upon as means to dissemble and put a gloss upon, rather than to discover . . . real sentiments." Smart quoted as prototypical of this mistaken former view a long section of Locke's discussion of "the Abuse of Words."[24] Smart responded by saying, "All words are originally tropes; that is, expressions *turned* (for such is the meaning of trope) from their first purpose, and extended to others."[25] He iterated the point: "When a particular name is enlarged to a general one, as our theory shows to have happened with all words now general, the change in the first instance was a trope."[26] It must not be assumed that figures and tropes "are ornaments superinduced on the plain matter of language, and capable of being detached from it: they are the original texture of language, and that from which whatever is now plain at first arose."[27]

Smart was not the first to make these claims, but the formidable backing he provided for his instrumental theory of contextual meaning gave his claims new force against views that treated figures and tropes as merely decorative and against theories of reading that cling to such views. I cite below a long passage from Smart's *Outline of Sematology* that exemplifies both the thoroughness of his arguments about meaning and figuration and the specific ways he applied his theory of tropes to explication of a text:

> These expedients are, in fact, essential parts of the original structure of language; and however they may sometimes serve the purposes of falsehood, they are, on most occasions, indispensable to the effective communication of truth. It is only by expedients that mind can unfold itself to mind;—language is made up of them; there is no such thing as an express and direct image of thought. Let a man's mind be penetrated with the clearest truth—let him burn to communicate the blessing to others;—yet can he, in no way, at once lay bare, nor can their minds at once receive, the truth as he is conscious of it. He therefore makes use of expedients:—he conceals, perhaps, his final purpose; for the mind which is to be informed, may not yet be ripe for it:—he has recourse to every form of comparison, (allegory, simile, metaphor,) by which he may awaken predisposing associations:—he changes one name for another, (metonymy,) connected with more agreeable, or more fa-

vourable associations:—he pretends to conceal what in fact he declares;—(apophasis;—) to pass by what in truth he reveals;—(paraleipsis:—) he interrogates when he wants no answer;—(erotesis;—) exclaims, when to himself there can be no sudden surprise;—(ecphonesis;—) he corrects an expression he designedly uttered;—(epanorthosis;—) he exaggerates;—(hyperbole;—) he gathers a number of particulars into one heap;—(synathroesmus;—) he ascends step by step to his strongest position;—(climax;—) he uses terms of praise in a sense quite opposite to their meaning;— (ironia;—) he personifies that which has no life, perhaps no sensible existence;—(prosopopoeia;—) he imagines he sees what is not actually present;—(hypotyposis;—) he calls upon the living and the dead;—(apostrophe;—) all these, and many more than these, are the artifices which the orator employs; but they are artifices which belong essentially to language; nor are there other means, taking them in their kind and not individually, by which men can be effectually *informed,* or *persuaded,* or *convinced.* Could the prophet at once have made the royal seducer of Uriah's wife fully conscious of the sin he had committed, he would not have approached him with a parable: that parable was the means of opening his heart and understanding to the true nature of his crime; and it is a proper instance of the principle on which all eloquence proceeds.[28]

Smart added to this discussion a note confirming his pragmatic perspective on figures and tropes:

In referring to these and other figures of speech, it is impossible not to be reminded of Butler's distich, that

All a rhetorician's rules
Teach nothing but to name his tools.

The fact is as the satirist states it. But then it is something to a workman to have a name for his tools; for this implies that he can find them handily.[29]

Smart's theory of reading as an art was based on recognition that writers do not "represent" their thoughts and feelings; they *strategically* manage commonly shared expedients of language that will make some *aspects* of their thought and feeling communicable. The expedients manipulated have to be "signs of knowledge we and our hearers have in common." These are adapted in form and usage to frame and suggest thoughts by means of linguistic "turns" that particular readers (or listeners) have "already attained." Not only does discourse *suggest* rather than *represent* thought and feeling, all means of such suggestion were in Smart's theory tropological. Smart had turned the old notion of style as "dress" on its head. He made linguistic management the "available means of persuasion." Management of verbal resources was a *rhetorical* action toward intended readers or listeners. A reader must therefore "read" the strategies as Smart "read" the prophet Nathan's parable told to King David. In one sense, at least, Smart had an answer to the old problem of how to discover authors' intentions: they were always rhetorical in that they always sought to "lead" readers in predetermined directions by means of tropologically adapted language.

As one looks at Smart's work in relation to that of his predecessors, it is plain that the pragmatic strain of reading theory and pedagogy had developed through several stages of evolution. By 1840 this pragmatic strain had made major strides toward what Toulmin might grant was a "discipline" of reading. The pragmatists, as opposed to the aestheticians, had repeatedly pondered the relationships of thought and language. Most pragmatists were favorably disposed toward rhetoric. They therefore presupposed that authors function *strategically* in composing discourses. As theorists of reading they looked for ways readers could discover the strategies and so grasp the "true" meanings of texts. This interest led the pragmatists from key-word views to a view of meaning that focused on all of the tropological strategies of language.

To move along such lines required, of course, that Locke's epistemological understandings of language and meaning be modified; and as the evidence has shown, all pragmatic theorists of reading did consciously modify Locke's analyses. In the first part of the nineteenth century Smart noted the positions of his pragmatic predecessors and found that they pointed toward a radically pragmatic interpretation of language *per se,* and he provided it.

To be sure, Smart left unsolved problems, some of which are being wrestled with today. For example, what is epistemologically implied by a figurationally based, instrumental view of contextual meaning? Paul de Man's work on the structures of figuration and epistemological models addresses some of the issues that Smart did not probe. And there were other philosophical, theoretical, and pedagogical problems about reading texts that Smart did not touch. Nonetheless, it is clear that by 1840 there existed in England a pragmatic theory of reading that had evolved through several generations of scholars and teachers. Yet the twentieth-century literature on reading largely disregards the suggestions and the trial-and-error lessons of these eighteenth-and early nineteenth-century struggles to evolve a sound theory of reading and to establish reading as a subject of study in and of itself.

Why did movement toward a discipline stop in 1840? Why did a rich one-hundred-thirty-year tradition of questions, answers, and debates about reading disappear, only to have many of the same basic questions reappear in the twentieth century? The answer lies deeply embedded in the history of nineteenth-century education in England and America, and in the histories of linguistics, literary criticism, and rhetoric. The disappearance deserves attention and research beyond the scope of this book; however, I want to briefly discuss one cause that has been implicit in my account of the history of reading theory and pedagogy. My emphasis in this chapter has been on the evolution of a *pragmatic* theory of what it is to read artfully—from my view the positive side of eighteenth- and nineteenth-century developments in reading theory and pedagogy. There was, however, a powerful counterview, the logic of which eventually led to a dismantling of the burgeoning systematic study of reading.

Several forces powered this counterview. There were the impulses toward romanticism variously manifested in John Dennis's higher criticism with its exaltation of genius, in John Mason's retreat to the older conception of style as "dress," in James Burgh's and Thomas Sheridan's utterance notion of contextual meaning, and especially in the ascendancy of Lord Kames's and Hugh Blair's aesthetic versions of critical reading. From the beginning these impulses existed within the overall pattern of reading studies. They also existed outside that framework, for belletrism, romanticism, and some versions of associational psychology reinforced notions that "taste," "genius," knowledge of proper "forms," and what Blair called meditation on the "viscera of the cause" were the true requisites for informed reading.

The two great exponents of the countering outlooks were, of course, George Campbell, whose pragmatic views were based for the most part on Humean psychology, and Blair, the leading spokesman for a belletristic view of human communication. Both men took the whole of verbal communication for their province; hence each represented the views he espoused in fuller form than did writers who concentrated exclusively on reading or oratory. The comparative force and tenacity of the pragmatic and the belletristic strands of theorizing can be seen by comparing the popularity in the eighteenth and nineteenth centuries of Campbell's and Blair's respected works on human communication. In the editor's introduction to Campbell's *Philosophy of Rhetoric*, Lloyd Bitzer was able to identify some fifty editions and printings of that book prior to 1912.[30] In contrast, Robert M. Schmitz, in his book on Hugh Blair, identified more than seventy full editions of the *Lectures on Rhetoric and Belles-Lettres,* all published before 1864![31] "No other book on rhetoric in English approaches a record of this kind, Harold F. Harding has rightly said of Blair's work.[32]

Blair and other belletrists represented a critical spirit and an approach to literature that undermined the case for an analytic, pragmatic theory of communication and pedagogy of reading. The popularity of Blair's *Lectures* dramatically indicates that the school of thought that he represented was overwhelmingly victorious in the nineteenth century. Insofar as Blair's *Lectures* dealt with reading, they offered *topics* for criticism of *style* (in the older sense) and of literary *forms*. Blair's major criterion for judgment of a verbal work was its conformity to "Nature" and to the "best usage of cultivated men"; he was the great popularizer of these standards for England and the United States.

Even the principles of associational psychology were modified to align with belletristic impulses. The nineteenth-century popularizer of this psychology as it was applied to communication was Alexander Bain.[33] To Bain the grammatical sentence and the paragraph constructed according to rule were the basic linguistic structures of communication. Their principles were set, unyielding, and defined "effectiveness" and "ineffectiveness." Bain extended Locke's epistemological premise to cover subunits of words joined. He gave "scientific credibility" to the idea that sentences and paragraphs are rule-governed structures and to the notion that if a composer attends to the propriety of his or her sentences and paragraphs, the essay as a whole will take care of itself. In short, discourse was made by putting linguistic blocks together according to culturally evolved rules of language. Bain's psychological discussions of how language is learned and used yielded a view of interpretation and critical reading that called for inspecting, describing, classifying, and naming the verbal patterns exhibited in a text. Here, we might say, was the ultimate triumph of the "philological" thrust in theory of communication—but it subjected only *form* to judgment. When qualitative judgments of the *substance* of a discourse came into question, Bain was consistent with Blair, saying this judgment must come from the reader's accumulated knowledge of the subject in question.

For studying any subject, including composition or criticism, Bain said, "an adequate familiarity with the great writers of the past both checks presumptuous or hasty efforts at reproduction, and encourages modest attempts of our own as we feel ourselves becoming gradually invigorated through the combined influence of all the various modes of well-directed study."[34] As a logician and psychologist, Bain arrived at the same sources of knowledge for critical reading that Blair recommended: the "laws" of language codify cultivated usage, and discourses are to be judged against those laws. Familiarity with the great writers of the past furnishes a reader with the criteria for evaluating the substance of what is said.

A theory of reading that presumed that one reads to find meaning beyond the expression and a "philological rhetoric" of "taste" and "correctness" together triumphed over rhetoric conceived as adaptive to discover clues to authorial meanings and strategies. This triumph is at least partially traceable to three developments: romanticism grew stronger through the latter part of the eighteenth century and the early part of the nineteenth century; the belletristic theory of communication was more attuned to that romantic spirit than was analytical, pragmatic theory; and popularizers of a nineteenth-century psychology of communication "authorized" non-analytical response to meanings *represented* through adherence to established forms.

NOTES TO CHAPTER 7

1. Benjamin Humphrey Smart, *The Theory of Elocution* (London: J. Richardson, 1819), p. iv. Frederick Haberman, "The Elocutionary Movement in England, 1750–1850," Ph.D. diss., Cornell University, 1947, provides a discussion of some of Smart's work in his survey "Manuals of Elocution," in which he finds Smart's to be "the most complete account of the theory of elocution, the best correlated account, and the most philosophical one of the period" (p. 360).
2. Smart, *Theory*, p. iv.
3. Benjamin Humphrey Smart, *An Outline of Sematology, or an Essay Towards Establishing a New Theory of Grammar, Logic, and Rhetoric* (London: J. Richardson, 1831), p. 2.
4. Smart, *Theory*, p. 4.
5. Smart, *Sematology*, p. 38.
6. Smart, *Sematology*, p. 6.
7. Smart, *Sematology*, pp. 9–10.
8. Smart, *Sematology*, p. 13.
9. Smart, *Sematology*, pp. 10–11.
10. Smart, *Sematology*, pp. 125, 183.
11. Smart, *Sematology*, p. 13.
12. Smart, *Sematology*, pp. 44–45.
13. Smart, *Sematology*, p. 50.
14. Smart, *Sematology*, p. 45.
15. I. A. Richards, *The Philosophy of Rhetoric* (New York: Oxford Unviersity Press, 1936), p. 31.
16. Smart, *Sematology*, p. 55.
17. Smart, *Sematology*, p. 54.

18. Smart, *Sematology,* p. 142.
19. Smart, *Sematology,* p. 247.
20. Richards, *Rhetoric,* p. 47.
21. Smart, *Sematology,* p. 184.
22. Smart, *Sematology,* p. 188.
23. Smart, *Sematology,* pp. 207–8.
24. Smart, *Sematology,* p. 208.
25. Smart, *Sematology,* p. 214.
26. Smart, *Sematology,* p. 214.
27. Smart, *Sematology,* p. 214.
28. Smart, *Sematology,* pp. 210ff.
29. Smart, *Sematology,* p. 211.
30. George Campbell, *The Philosophy of Rhetoric,* ed. L. Bitzer (1776; reprint, Carbondale: Southern Illinois University Press, 1963), pp. xxx–xxxi.
31. Robert M. Schmitz, *Hugh Blair* (Morningside Heights, N.Y.: King's Crown Press, 1948), pp. 144–45.
32. Hugh Blair, *Lectures on Rhetoric and Belles-Lettres,* ed. Harold F. Harding (1783; reprint, Carbondale: Southern Illinois University Press, 1965), vol. 1, p. xxxvii.
33. Alexander Bain, *Manual of English Composition and Rhetoric* (London: Longmans, Green, 1866). See also the 1887 revision by the same publisher.
34. Alexander Bain, "The Art of Study," in *Practical Essays* (London: Longmans and Co., 1884), p. 254.

# 8

# RECALLING FORGOTTEN
# LESSONS FOR THE FUTURE
# OF READING

The history of studies of reading between 1710 and 1840 tells a story within a story. The context for the discussions among reading theorists during this period was one of controversy, often heated, concerning the nature of human communication and of art. A fundamental issue was: Where do the most important "secrets" concerning human communication lie? In the eighteenth and early nineteenth centuries grammarians, logicians, rhetoricians, literary critics, and philosophers addressed this question from many vantage points, but their answers tended to fall into one of two general classes. One kind of answer asserted or implied that in communication the secrets, or meanings, arise from observance of established principles of the *code*. The other kind of answer asserted or implied that the secrets or meanings lie in *strategies* purposively chosen to build particular kinds of *human relationships* with specific kinds of readers or listeners. Both kinds of answers informed the work of these writers on reading.

The early reading theorists were trying to understand and teach the whole nature of language. They did not progress far enough to understand fully the important distinctions that Jerold J. Katz has emphasized in the twentieth century:

A theory of linguistics explicates linguistic competence, not linguistic performance. It seeks to reconstruct the logical structure of the principles that speakers have mastered in attaining fluency. On the other hand, a theory of performance seeks to discover the contribution of each of the factors that interplay to produce natural speech with its various and sundry deviations from ideal linguistic forms.

Thus it must consider such linguistically extraneous factors as memory span, perceptual and motor limitations, lapses of attention, pauses, level of motivation, interest, idiosyncratic and random errors, etc.[1]

Put in Katz's terms, some answers offered by eighteenth-and early nineteenth-century writers on reading derived from theories of "linguistic competence" and some derived from theories of "performance." In more traditional terms, some of these writers gave philological-aesthetic answers and some derived their answers from pragmatic conceptions of "rhetorical grammar."

A congeries of philosophical, literary, psychological, and other forces rendered linguistic-philological-aesthetic answers popular and eventually muted the voices of pragmatic, performance theorists and theorists of rhetorical grammar. This affected study of composition, literary criticism, and aesthetics generally, with the result that reading as a practical art virtually ceased to hold interest for students of verbal communication until well into the twentieth century.

The philosophical differences that divided eighteenth-and early nineteenth-century reading theorists extend to our own time. Theories of reading as disparate as those represented in "new criticism" and "reader-response criticism" have arisen to counter "scientific" and positivist conceptions of language. Jane Tompkins has made the point that although their strategies are radically different, "response-centered critical theory is engaged in exactly the same power struggle with science that played so large a role in the formation of new Critical doctrine."[2]

Because controversy about how meaning is to be discovered in language is still with us, the eighteenth-and nineteenth-century explorations of reading are especially instructive, for through them we can see what issues must be resolved if the points of controversy are to be clear or if a consensus is to emerge. The early theorists uncovered fundamental questions that any theory of reading must answer:

1. What are the relationships between thought and language?
2. Can one legitimately posit epistemological and psychological formulations *prior* to analyzing the practical workings of language?
3. How do the spoken and written forms of language interrelate, i.e., what are the common and the distinctive communicative potentialities of each form?
4. Are reading for comprehension and critical reading separable activities?

5. To what extent is it feasible or desirable to try to discover authorial meanings from texts?
6. What verbal forms or structures are reliable guides to the meanings of written discourse, and do these guides vary in meaningfulness generically or situationally?
7. Are there forms or structures that convey meanings consistently across genres and situations for all authors using a given language?

Eighteenth- and early nineteenth-century students of reading confronted these questions and frequently disagreed about the answers to them. They are questions on which every aspiring reading theorist must take a stand. Each, in turn, thrusts a thinker back to the root question, where do the secrets concerning human communication lie?

As my study illustrates, one's answers to the root question and to its subordinate questions will determine what one can and will outline as the *art* of reading well. Among other things, one must be able to say *who* gives the significant meanings to human communication. Does meaning lie in the features an author gives to the communication, or does meaning arise from the nature and capacities of the person perceiving it?

Historically and at present there have been many people who have agreed with Lord Kames:

What a man feels distinctly to be beautiful, is beautiful for him, whatever other people may think of it . . . . [B]ut it does not follow . . . that all tastes are equally good, or desirable, or that there is any difficulty in describing that which is really the best, and the most to be envied . . . . The best taste . . . must be that which belongs to the best affections, the most active fancy, and the most attentive habits of observation. It will follow pretty exactly too, that all men's perceptions of beauty will be nearly in proportion to the degree of their sensibility and social sympathies; and that those who have no affections towards sentient beings, will be as certainly insensible to beauty in external objects, as he who cannot bear the sound of his friend's voice, must be deaf to its echo.[3]

Such views invoking taste, sensitivity, or some other abstract quality of a perceiver's mind cannot propose a pedagogy of reading for all persons. No one holding such views in the eighteenth and early nineteenth centuries proposed any but the most general ways of improving citizens' capacities to learn from and enjoy the printed word. Nor is it likely that anyone holding comparable views today would be able to present a specific way to teach people to read well.

The pragmatists among the early reading theorists had a very different outlook and, therefore, radically different views on how reading could and should be improved. For example, about even so abstract a notion as taste, Joseph Priestley said:

> Judgment is universally acknowledged to be altogether acquired, and that *taste,* too, or the capacity of perceiving the pleasures of imagination, may also be acquired, to a very great degree, is evident from the actual acquirement of a variety of similar tastes, even late in life. Instances of this may be given in a taste for flowers, for gardening, and for architecture, which are hardly ever acquired very early in life . . . . Besides, it will appear very clearly in our progress through this subject [criticism], that all the *principles of taste* in works of genius, the very sources from which all these fine pleasures are derived, are within the reach of all persons whatsoever; and that scarce any person can pass his life in cultivated society, where the fine arts flourish, without acquiring, in a greater or a less degree, a taste for some or other of them.[4]

Even aesthetic appreciation could be *learned,* according to Priestley. The other pragmatists agreed that even the sources of pleasures of the imagination "are within the reach of all persons." If this is true of aesthetic appreciation, how much more true it must be for the principles of an art of reading for comprehension!

Any attempt to explain what it is to read well will reflect some view of how far *nurture* can improve native or innate abilities. The experience of the eighteenth and nineteenth centuries indicates that only those who have confidence in nurture will be motivated to propose and forward systematic programs for improving skills in reading.

The pragmatic reading theorists' successes in borrowing from rhetorical theory between 1710 and 1840 should give heart to those who today explore what Geoffrey Hartman describes as the "theory of convention, as it rules both reading and writing," now being studied by persons "who are presently expanding and rationalizing the historical study of rhetoric . . . on the level of poetics."[5] Such investigators should take encouragement from those who, two centuries ago, saw principles of *adaptive* figuration in rhetorical theory and thus were the ones who came closest to a comprehensive theory of reading.

I hope my study contributes to a revised view of the British rhetorical tradition in the eighteenth and early nineteenth centuries, for in at least three respects my account differs from standard accounts of rhetoric in Great Britain. First a practical kind of rhetoric did coexist, even at pedagogical levels, with the much-discussed aesthetic, Longinian rhetorical theories. Second, a number of neglected writers contributed significant ideas about rhetorical communication, especially in modifying Locke's epistemological model. Numbered among those forgotten figures were Isaac Watts, who is too often remembered only as a theologian and hymn writer; Robert Lowth, who is remembered largely as a theological scholar; John Rice and William Cockin, whose names do not even appear in standard works on eighteenth-century rhetoric; John Walker, whose elocutionist activities have been allowed to overshadow his equally serious thoughts concerning language and rhetoric; and Benjamin Smart, who is also treated (if at all) as an elocutionist, despite his forward-looking expansions of inherited theory of reading. All of these writers borrowed significantly from what was essentially a practical, Ciceronian rhetoric—especially as that strand of rhetorical theory treated figuration as strategic and arrangement as strategic *dispositio*. I also have shown that the treatment of Hugh Blair as a man professing a full-bodied rhetorical system is at best questionable, and that the belletristic tradition in rhetoric added little to the useful body of rhetorical theory and virtually nothing to practical pedagogy in reading.

Third, in addition to rescuing some constructive rhetorical thinkers from obscurity, I have shown that a new concept of style emerged in what I have called the pragmatic strain of reading theory. This movement toward a conception of style as rhetorical strategy has been almost totally ignored in accounts of eighteenth-century rhetorical theory in Great Britain. Its special importance for theory of reading was that it posited figuration as a body of persuasive strategies that were open to analysis and could reveal authorial intentions. Because of the ultimate dominance of belletristic theory, the pragmatic conception of figuration was not restored to theory of language until the mid-twentieth century, when it appeared in works such as Chaim Perelman and L. Olbrechts-Tyteca's *The New Rhetoric: A Treatise on Argumentation* and the writings of Paul de Man on critical reading.[6]

Whether reading is, can be, or should be considered a subject to be studied independently of other subjects remains an open question today, as it was in the 1840s. However, between 1710 and 1840 there was progress toward a comprehensive theory of reading that defined reading as an art deserving treatment in much the same way as composition, which is often treated as an art independent of others. The major questions I have set forth must be answered if we are to treat reading as an

149

explicable art, which I believe it is. The lesson of the eighteenth and early nineteenth centuries is that the first step in this direction must be to accept the reality that authors write, or think they are writing, *adaptively* in describable and discussable ways for readers whom they have conceptualized. Writers do not just *express;* they try to *communicate,* and we as readers should study their *strategic* moves for information about their "designs." If this is not true, then reading cannot be a democratized activity and must be the special privilege of an elite blessed with genius, taste, and extrasensory perceptions.

NOTES TO CHAPTER 8

1. Jerrold J. Katz, "The Philosophical Relevance of Linguistic Theory," *Journal of Philosophy* 62 (1965): 590–602.

2. Jane Tompkins, "The Reader in History," in *Reader Response Criticism,* ed. Jane Tompkins (Baltimore, Md.: The Johns Hopkins University Press, 1980), p. 224.

3. Lord Kames, [Henry Home], *Elements of Criticism* (New York: A. S. Barnes and Co., 1855), p. 128.

4. Joseph Priestley, *A Course of Lectures on Oratory and Criticism,* ed. V. Bevilacqua and R. Murphy (1777; reprint, Carbondale: Southern Illinois University Press, 1965), p. 74.

5. Geoffrey H. Hartman, *The Fate of Reading* (Chicago: University of Chicago Press, 1977), p. 273.

6. Chaim Perelman and L. Olbrechts-Tyteca, *The New Rhetoric: A Treatise on Argumentation* (Notre Dame, Ind.: Notre Dame University Press, 1969).

# NAME INDEX

# Name Index

Haberman, Frederick, 143n
Harding, Harold F., 142
Hartley, David, 105
Hartman, Geoffrey, 9, 10n, 30, 34n, 148, 150n
Hawkes, Terrence, 31, 34n
Hirsch, E. D., Jr., 4, 8, 10n, 116, 129n
Hobbes, Thomas, 38
Home, Henry (Lord Kames), 89, 91, 99–105, 106, 108n, 141–142, 147, 150n
Hooker, Edward Niles, 66
Hoole, Charles, 13
Hoskins, John, 20
Howell, Wilbur Samuel, 3, 10n, 45–46, 66n, 108n
Howes, Raymond F., 33
Hume, David, 56, 66n, 78
Hutcheson, Francis, 56, 105

Jakobson, Roman, 9, 30–31, 122, 134
Jennings, D., 65
Johnson, Samuel, 37, 52
Jones, M. G., 12, 33n

Kames. *See* Home, Henry
Katz, Jerold J., 145–146, 150n
Kemp, J. A., 34n
Kenrick, William, 124–126, 129n
Kitchin, G. W., 33n
Kretzmann, Norman, 34n
Kuster, Ludolph, 55

Land, Stephen K., 2, 5, 10n
Lessing, Gotthold E., 9
Levine, Joseph M., 15, 33n
Linacer, Thomas, 29
Locke, John, 8, 10n, 20, 23–24, 36–40, 45, 46, 50–51, 52, 55, 58, 63–64, 69, 78, 79–80, 83, 91, 132, 133, 134, 138, 140, 142, 149
Longinus, 55, 57, 59, 89, 92, 99, 104, 105, 149
Lowth, Robert, 89–94, 105, 107–108n, 111, 116, 118, 121, 123, 127, 149

MacIllmaine, Roland, 17
MacLean, Norman, 92, 107n
Maittaire, Michael, 25, 30

Manley, Lawrence, 20, 33n, 46, 66n
Mason, John, 69–76, 76n, 77, 78, 80, 81, 84, 85, 86, 91, 94, 100, 141
Miller, George A., 3–4, 10n
Monk, Samuel, 92, 107n
Morris, David, 64–65, 67n
Murphy, Richard, 105, 108n

Olbrechts-Tyteca, L., 149, 150n
Ong, Walter, 8, 10n, 33n, 75, 76n
Ortony, Andrew, 10n

Parker, Irene, 33n
Perelman, Chaim, 149, 150n
Plato, 86
Pope, Alexander, 14, 54–55, 59, 66n, 73, 120
Pratt, Anne S., 65n
Priestley, Joseph, 13, 89–91, 94–97, 99, 105, 106, 107, 108–109n, 111, 112, 115, 121, 123, 127, 136, 138, 148, 150n
Puttenham, George, 20, 28, 34n, 46

Quintilian, 29

Ramus, Peter, 16–17, 47–48, 58
Reid, Thomas, 91
Rice, John, 111–114, 115, 116, 117, 121, 122, 123, 124, 125, 126, 127, 128, 128–129n, 133, 149
Richards, I. A., 133, 134, 136, 137, 143n, 144n

Sacks, Sheldon, 66n
Sanctius (F. Sanchez de las Brozas), 29
Saussure, Ferdinand de, 30, 86
Scaglione, Aldo, 19, 29, 33n, 34n
Schmitz, Robert M., 142, 144n
Selby-Bigge, L. A., 66n
Sheridan, Thomas, 42, 77–87, 87–88n, 91, 94, 100, 104, 111, 112, 113, 114, 114–115, 117, 123, 124, 126–127, 129n, 141
Sherry, Richard, 20
Sloane, Thomas O., 10n
Smart, Benjamin Humphrey, 131–140, 143n, 144n
Smith, John, 28, 34n

152

# SUBJECT INDEX

Ancients-versus-moderns controversy or the battle of the books, 11, 14–16, 64. *See also* Philology; Critical reading
Antithesis. *See* Rhetoric
Arrangement (method or *dispositio*). *See* Rhetoric

Basic reading or reading for comprehension, 2–5, 11–14, 18; relation to critical reading, 2–4, 14–16, 35–36, 50–52, 57–60, 71–72, 77, 106–107, 111, 127–128
Biblical interpretation, 31–33, 49–50, 57–58, 91, 98–99. *See also* Critical reading; Philology

Classicism versus romanticism, 15–16, 89, 104–107. *See also* Critical reading; Philology; Taste; Sublimity
Competence-performance distinction, 86–87, 145–146
Contextual meaning. *See* Meaning
Critical reading or literary criticism, 4–5, 9, 14–16, 50–52, 54–65; pragmatic versions, 35–54, 89–99, 131–143; belletristic versions, 54–65, 95–96, 99–107, 141–143. *See also* Basic reading
Criticism. *See* Critical reading
Customary use: viewed as including figurative language, 8–9, 19–20, 38–42, 45–47, 64–65, 95–96, 97–98, 103, 122–123, 134–135; viewed as excluding figurative language, 20–21, 45–47, 64–65, 102–103

Education. *See* Schools and reading
Ellipsis. *See* Rhetoric
Emphasis, rhetorical versus linguistic, 28–29, 43–44, 81–83, 113, 122–123, 125–126
Epistemology: the Lockean model and responses to it, 9, 35–38, 64–65, 77, 78–80, 91, 97, 133, 140; and meaning, 9, 21–22, 38–41, 45–47, 50, 78–80, 133–143. *See also* Meaning; Language and thought

Figures and tropes. *See* Rhetoric

Genre, 96–97, 99
Grammar, 16, 22–31, 52, 114–128; and syntax, 29–31, 90–91, 113–114, 117–123; and rhetoric, 27, 30–31, 118–128; the study of reading as a supplement to, 25–27, 52. *See also* Rhetorical grammar; Rhetoric

Instrumental view of contextual meaning. *See* Meaning

Key-word view of contextual meaning. *See* Meaning

Language and thought, separability or inseparability of, 18–22, 38–41, 90–99. *See also* Meaning; Style
Language theory. *See* Meaning; Epistemology; Style; Language and thought
Langue-parole distinction, 19, 86–87

154

# Subject Index

Linguistics. *See* Spoken language versus written language; Philology; Meaning; Language and thought; Competence-performance distinction; Langue-parole distinction; Emphasis

Linguistic emphasis. *See* Emphasis

Literary criticism. *See* Critical reading or literary criticism; Philology

Meaning, 3, 8, 22–24; referential theories of, 22–23, 24; ideational theories of, 23–24; utterance notion of, 69–76, 77–87; instrumental view of, 131–143; sentence view of, 111–128; key-word view of, 41–54; I. A. Richards' interinanimation view of, 133, 134, 135–138; and figurative language, 27–29, 92–99, 131–143; and grammar, 9, 22–24; and style, 24. *See also* Language and thought; Epistemology; Rhetoric

Metaphor. *See* Rhetoric

Metonymy. *See* Rhetoric

New criticism, 146

Oral reading versus silent reading, 7–8, 42–44, 81. *See also* Spoken language versus written language

Ordinary language, 31–32

Philology, 14–16, 31–33, 54–55, 57–58, 61, 92–93. *See also* Ancients-versus-moderns controversy; Critical reading; Biblical interpretation

Psychology, 1, 2, 105–107, 141–142, 146. *See also* Epistemology; Meaning

Punctuation, 71–72, 81–82, 118, 126

Ramistic tradition, 16–18, 20, 47–48, 58, 97

Reader-response criticism, 146

Reading: definitions of, 3–5; interdisciplinary nature of reading theory, 1–2, 5–9, 11, 16. *See also* Basic reading, Critical reading, Reading material

Reading material and demand for reading instruction, 11–14

Rhetoric, 7, 8–9, 15, 17, 45–47, 49, 63, 69–70, 77, 99, 153, 148–149; figures and tropes, 8–9, 18–22, 27–29, 38–40, 45–47, 63–65, 87, 91, 94–98, 102–104, 119–123, 133–143, 148–149: antithesis, 29, 41–42, 45, 73, 87, 95, 119–122, ellipsis, 29, 119–123, metaphor, 30, 40–41, 60, 63, 95, 98, 103, 123, 134, 138, metonymy, 30, 98, 134, 138, elliptical opposition versus overt opposition, 119–121; arrangement (method or *dispositio*), 16–18, 47–49, 64, 136–137, 149; style, 8–9, 18–22, 24, 45–47, 64, 72–73, 90–91, 148–149

Rhetorical emphasis. *See* Emphasis

Rhetorical grammar, 26, 29, 123–128. *See also* Rhetoric

Romanticism. *See* Classicism versus romanticism; Sublimity; Taste; Critical reading

Royal Society, 22, 25, 36, 38

Schools and reading instruction before the eighteenth century, 12–14; charity schools, 13; petty schools, 13; dissenting academies, 13

Semantics. *See* Meaning; Epistemology

Sentence view of contextual meaning. *See* Meaning

Speech act theory, 134

Spoken language versus written language, 3, 7–8, 26–29, 42–44, 53, 69–76, 80–87, 111–128, 132–133. *See also* Oral reading versus silent reading

Style. *See* Rhetoric

Sublimity, 59–63, 64–65, 92–93, 99–105. *See also* Taste; Critical reading

Syntax. *See* Grammar

Taste, 14, 56–57, 64–65, 71–72, 78, 89, 92, 99–105, 117–118, 121, 141, 147, 148, 150. *See also* Sublimity; Critical reading

Utterance notion of contextual meaning. *See* Meaning

155